Prehistoric villages, castles, and towers of southwestern

Jesse Walter Fewkes

Alpha Editions

This edition published in 2024

ISBN 9789361472527

Design and Setting By

Alpha Editions
www.alphaedis.com

Email - info@alphaedis.com

As per information held with us this book is in Public Domain.
This book is a reproduction of an important historical work.
Alpha Editions uses the best technology to reproduce historical work
in the same manner it was first published to preserve its original nature.
Any marks or number seen are left intentionally to preserve.

Contents

INTRODUCTION .... - 1 -

HISTORICAL .... - 3 -

CLASSIFICATION .... - 8 -

VILLAGES .... - 9 -

CLIFF-DWELLINGS .... - 30 -

GREAT HOUSES AND TOWERS .... - 33 -

MEGALITHIC AND SLAB HOUSE RUINS AT MCELMO BLUFF ... - 55 -

GRASS MESA CEMETERY .... - 60 -

RESERVOIRS .... - 61 -

PICTOGRAPHS .... - 62 -

MINOR ANTIQUITIES .... - 64 -

HISTORIC REMAINS .... - 66 -

CONCLUSIONS .... - 67 -

INDEX .... - 75 -

INTRODUCTION

The science of archeology has contributed to our knowledge some of the most fascinating chapters in culture history, for it has brought to light, from the night of the past, periods of human development hitherto unrecorded. As the paleontologist through his method has revealed faunas whose like were formerly unknown to the naturalist, the archeologist by the use of the same method of research has resurrected extinct phases of culture that have attained a high development and declined before recorded history began. No achievements in American anthropology are more striking than those that, from a study of human buildings and artifacts antedating the historic period, reveal the existence of an advanced prehistoric culture of man in America.

The evidences of a phase of culture that had developed and was on the decline before the interior of North America was explored by Europeans are nowhere better shown than in southwestern Colorado, New Mexico, Arizona, and Utah, the domain of the Cliff-dwellers, or the cradle of the Pueblos. There flourished on what is now called the Mesa Verde National Park, in prehistoric times, a characteristic culture unlike that of any region in the United States. This culture reached its apogee and declined before the historic epoch, but did not perish before it had left an influence extending over a wide territory, which persisted into modern times. Through the researches of archeologists the nature of this culture is now emerging into full view; but much material yet remains awaiting investigation before it can be adequately understood. The purpose of this article is to call attention to new observations bearing upon its interpretation made by the author, under the auspices of the Bureau of American Ethnology, on brief trips to Colorado and Utah in 1917 and 1918.

The peculiar cliff-dwellings and open-air villages of the Mesa Verde are here shown to be typical of those found over a region many miles in extent. They indicate a distinct culture area, which is easily distinguished from others where similar buildings do not exist, but not as readily separated from that of adjacent regions where the buildings are superficially similar but structurally different. In order to distinguish it from its neighbors and determine its horizon, we must become familiar with certain architectural characteristics. As our knowledge of the character of buildings in this area is incomplete, the intention of the author is to define the several different types of buildings that characterize it.

When, in 1915, there was brought to light on the Mesa Verde National Park, Colorado, the mysterious structure, Sun Temple, the author recalled well-known descriptions of towers and other related buildings that have been recorded from other localities in southwestern Colorado and Utah. The published descriptions of these structures did not seem to him adequate for comparisons, and he planned an examination of these great houses and towers, hoping to gather new data that would shed some light on his interpretation of Sun Temple. During the field work in 1917, thanks to an allotment from the Bureau of American Ethnology for that purpose, he undertook a reconnoissance in the McElmo district, where similar buildings are found and where he believed cultural relatives of the former inhabitants of Mesa Verde once lived. In 1918 he extended his field work still farther. He investigated ruins as far as the western tributaries of the Yellow Jacket Canyon, penetrating a short distance beyond the Colorado border into Utah. The object of the following pages is to make known the more important results of this visit, and interpret the evidence they present as a contribution to our knowledge of the extension in prehistoric times of the Mesa Verde culture area.

HISTORICAL

Attention was first publicly called, about 40 years ago (1875-1877), by Messrs. Jackson,[1] Holmes, Morgan, and others, to some of the ruins here considered. It is difficult to identify all of the ruins mentioned or described by these pioneers. Their "Hovenweep Castle" is supposed to lie in about the center of the district here considered, possibly on Square Tower (Ruin) Canyon, although the large castellated building[2] in Holly Canyon would also fulfill conditions equally well. Their "Pueblo" may have been situated on the McElmo near the mouth of Yellow Jacket Canyon. Early writers rather vaguely refer to a cluster of castles and towers as situated some distance from the "Burial Place," which is readily identified on the promontory at the mouth of the McElmo, as probably those in Square Tower (Ruin) Canyon, but the cluster may be either at Square Tower or Holly Canyon, both of which are about the same distance from this site. As "Pueblo" is not indicated on the map accompanying the Hayden report, the sites of rock shelters "some 7 miles from 'Pueblo' and 3 miles from the McElmo" remain doubtful. The author retains the name "Hovenweep Castle" for the ruin in Square Tower Canyon.

In his account of ruins in the region visited, Prof. W. H. Holmes[3] considers several other ruins, as "the triple-walled tower" (here called Mud Spring village, p. 20), ruins at Aztec Spring (p. 23), cliff-dwellings and towers of the San Juan and Mancos, the "slab cysts" or burial places on the Dolores, and the promontory at the junction of the Hovenweep and McElmo (p. 60). The best preserved towers and castellated buildings which his article considers occur on the San Juan and Mancos Canyons, districts on the periphery of the region covered by this account.

These pioneer reports of Jackson and Holmes not only called attention to a new archeological field, but also introduced to the archeologist several new types of prehistoric American architecture of which nothing was previously known. They have been repeatedly quoted and are still constantly referred to by writers on southwestern archeology.

Although Jackson made many photographs of the castles and towers of the Hovenweep, none of these were published in his reports, possibly because halftone methods of reproduction were then unknown. The illustrations that appear in the text of early reports are mainly reproductions of sketches. These reports, in which the discovery of the tower type of architecture and its adjacent cliff-dwellings were announced, should thus rightly rank as the first important steps in the scientific investigations of the stone-house builders of this district of our Southwest; although the allied "Casas Grandes" or great houses of the Chaco had been described a few years before by Gregg, Stimpson, and others.

We have, in addition to these pioneer reports, several magazine articles of about the same date, the material for which was largely drawn from them. One of the most important newspaper articles of that date was written by Mr. Ernest Ingersoll, published in the New York Tribune, and another, of anonymous authorship, is to be found in the Century Magazine for the year 1877. New forms of towers and castellated buildings were added in these accounts to those of the earlier authors.

One of the most important contributions to the antiquities of the region about Mesa Verde was made by the veteran ethnologist, Morgan, who published notes contributed by Mr. Mitchell on a cluster of mounds near his ranch. As no name was given this village it is here called the Mitchell Spring Village. Morgan likewise mentions the ruin at Mud Spring and a tower in the ruin near his spring. Professor Newberry was the first author to affix the name Surouaro to a ruin situated at the head of the Yellow Jacket Canyon.

Several of these ruins were described and figured by Mr. Warren K. Moorehead as "The Great Ruins of Upper McElmo Creek" in the Illustrated American for July 9, 1892, the sixth of a series of articles under a general title "In search of a Lost Race." He gives descriptions of a "cave shelter" found near Twin Towers, Square Tower in "Ruin Canyon," a building (Hovenweep Castle), and the tower at the junction of the North and South Forks of Ruin Canyon. This paper is accompanied by a map of Ruin Canyon by Mr. Cowen. In Moorehead's discussion of these remains, individual towers and other ruins are designated by capital letters, A-V, to some of which are also affixed the names "Hollow Boulder," "Twin Towers," "Square Tower," etc. Details of structure and measurements of the more striking buildings and a discussion of certain features of structure, some of which will be considered later under individual ruins, are likewise given.

The most important general article yet published on the prehistoric remains of the region here considered is by Dr. T. Mitchell Prudden,[4] who also mentions several of the ruins here treated. His most important contribution is a description of what he calls the "unit type," which he recognized as a fundamental structural feature in the pueblos of this region. He also showed that the kiva in Montezuma Valley villages is identical with that of cliff-dwellings in the Mesa Verde, and emphasized, as an important feature, the union of the tower and the pueblo, a characteristic of the highest form of pueblo architecture.

Doctor Prudden has followed his comprehensive paper above mentioned with an account[5] of the excavation of one of the mounds at Mitchell Spring in which he adds to our knowledge of the structure of his "unit type."

In "A Further Study of Prehistoric Small House Ruins in the San Juan Watershed,"[6] Doctor Prudden has furnished important additional data which shows the uniformity of the unit type over a large area of the San Juan drainage.

The following among other prehistoric remains in the district mentioned or described by Doctor Prudden are covered by the author's reconnoissance:

- 1. Ruins at Dolores Bend (Escalante Ruin).
- 2. Wolley Ranch Ruin.
- 3. Burkhardt Ruin (Mud Spring Village).
- 4. Goodman Point Ruin.
- 5. Unnamed ruin west of Goodman Lake.
- 6. Ruin at junction of McElmo and Yellow Jacket.
- 7. Group on Yellow Jacket nearly opposite mouth of Dawson Canyon
    - (Davis or Littrell Tower).
- 8. Surouaro.
- 9. Cannonball Ruin.
- 10. Towers and buildings of Ruin and Bridge Canyons.
- 11. Pierson Spring Ruin.
- 12. Bug Spring Ruins.

The following towers can be identified from his figures:[7]

1. "Square building opposite mouth of Dawson Creek." Prudden, pl. xviii, fig. 2. (This building is not square, but semicircular.)
2. Cannonball Ruin. Prudden, pl. xxi [xxii].
3. "Small tower-like structure ... at the head of Ruin Canyon, in the Yellow Jacket group." Prudden, pl. xxiii, fig. 2. (This building is not in Ruin Canyon, but in Holly Canyon.)

4. "Tower ... about the head of Ruin Canyon." Prudden, pl. xxiii, fig. 1. (This is the most eastern of the Twin Towers, but not about the head of the canyon.)

5. Sand Canyon Tower. Prudden, pl. xxiv, fig. 2.

Although mainly devoted to descriptions of the cliff-houses of the Mesa Verde, Baron G. Nordenskiöld's "Cliff-Dwellers of the Mesa Verde" discusses in so broad a manner the relationship of pueblo ruins and cliff-houses that no student can overlook this epoch-making work. In fact, Nordenskiöld laid the foundations for subsequent students of pueblo morphology, although some of his comparisons and generalizations were premature because based on imperfect observations which have been superseded by later investigations.

The partial excavation of the excellent ruin at the head of Cannonball Canyon by S. G. Morley[8] sheds considerable light on the morphology of prehistoric buildings in the McElmo district. Unfortunately no attempt was made by him to repair the walls of this ruin for permanent preservation, but it is not too late still to prevent their further destruction and preserve them for future students and visitors. Morley's description of the buildings is accompanied by good photographs and a ground plan. He brought to light in this ruin examples of the characteristic unit type kiva.

The latest work on the McElmo Ruins, one part of which has already appeared, is a joint contribution by Morley and Kidder.[9] In this publication accurate dimensions and sites of ruins in the McElmo and Square Ruin Canyons are given, with other instructive data. Morley and Kidder have designated the ruins by Arabic numbers, and in a few instances by names. The author has preserved these numbers so far as possible in his account.

The following ruins in Ruin Canyon and neighboring district covered by this reconnoissance are described by Morley and Kidder:

- No. 1. Wickyup Canyon, Ruin 1 and Ruin 2, "Boulder Castle."
- No. 2. Two towers in Ruin Canyon: 1□, near the mouth; 1□,
    - Towers on or near forks, No. 1 [Hovenweep Pueblo],
    - No. 2 [Hovenweep Castle.]
- No. 3. [Square Tower.]
- No. 4. [Oval Tower.]
- No. 5. [Tower.]
- No. 6. [6.]

- No. 7. [Boulder Cliff-house.]
- No. 8. Twin Towers.
- No. 9. [9.]
- No. 10. [Unit type House.]
- No. 11. Gibraltar House and ruin. [Stronghold House.]
- No. 12. [12.]

The pueblos and cave dwellings of the "Pivotal group" (those on or near the promontory at the junction of the McElmo and Yellow Jacket Canyons) were also studied by the authors.

Almost the whole article by Morley and Kidder, which the editor announces will be completed in a future number of "El Palacio," is devoted to descriptions of buildings[10] in Ruin and Road (Wickyup) Canyons and the ruins of the "Pivotal group" at the base of a promontory between the junction of the Yellow Jacket and McElmo.

CLASSIFICATION

In the classification by Morley and Kidder and the majority of writers, sites rather than structural features are adopted as a basis although all recognized that large cliff-dwellings like Cliff Palace are practically pueblos built in caves. In the following classification more attention is directed to differences in structure than to situation, notwithstanding the latter is convenient for descriptive purposes.

1. Villages or clusters of houses, each having the form of the pure pueblo type. The essential feature of the pure type is a compact pueblo, containing one or more unit types, circular kivas of characteristic form, surrounded by rectangular rooms. These units, single or consolidated, may be grouped in clusters, as Mitchell Spring or Aztec Spring Ruins; the clusters may be fused into a large building, as at Aztec or in the community buildings on Chaco Canyon.

2. Cliff-houses. These morphologically belong to the same pure type as pueblos; their sites in natural caves are insufficient to separate them from open-sky buildings.

3. Towers and great houses. These buildings occur united to cliff-dwellings or pueblos, but more often they are isolated.

4. Rooms with walls made of megaliths or small stone slabs set on edge.

In reports on the excavation of Far View House[11] on the Mesa Verde, the author called attention to clusters of mounds indicating ruined buildings in the neighborhood of Mummy Lake, a little more than 4 miles from Spruce-tree House. This cluster he considers a village; Far View House, excavated from one of the mounds, is regarded as a prehistoric pueblo of the pure type. The forms of other buildings covered by the remaining mounds of the Mummy Lake site are unknown, but it is probable that they will be found to resemble Far View House, or that all members of the village have similar forms.

This grouping of small pueblos into villages at Mummy Lake on the Mesa Verde is also a distinctive feature of ruins in the Montezuma Valley and McElmo district. In these villages one or more of the component houses may be larger and more conspicuous, dominating all the others, as at Goodman Point, or at Aztec Spring. The houses composing the village at Mud Spring were about the same size, but at Wolley Ranch Ruin only one mound remains, evidently the largest, the smaller having disappeared.

The third group, towers and great houses, includes buildings of oval, circular, semicircular, and rectangular shapes. Morphologically speaking, they do not present structural features of pueblos, for they are not terraced, neither have they specialized circular ceremonial rooms, kivas with vaulted roofs surrounded by rectangular rooms, or other essential features of the pueblo type. The group contains buildings which are sometimes consolidated with cliff-houses and pueblos, but are often independent of them. In this type are included castellated buildings in the Mancos, Yellow Jacket, McElmo, and the numerous northern tributary canyons of the San Juan.

Villages

RECTANGULAR RUINS OF THE PURE TYPE

As the word is used in this report, a village is a cluster of houses separated from each other, each building constructed on the same plan, viz, a circular ceremonial room or kiva with mural banquettes and pilasters for the support of a vaulted roof, inclosed in rectangular rooms. When there is one kiva and surrounding angular rooms we adopt the name "unit type." When, as in the larger mounds, there are indications of several kivas or unit types consolidated—the size being in direct proportion to the number—we speak of the building as belonging to the "pure type." Doctor Prudden, who first pointed out the characteristics of the "unit type,"[12] has shown its wide distribution in the McElmo district. The Mummy Lake village has 16 mounds indicating houses. Far View House, one of these houses, is made up of an aggregation of four unit types and hence belongs to the author's "pure type."

While villages similar to the Mummy Lake group, in the valleys near Mesa Verde, have individual variations, the essential features are the same, as will appear in the following descriptions of Surouaro, and ruins at Goodman Point, Mud Spring, Aztec Spring, and Mitchell Spring. Commonly, in these villages, one mound predominates in size over the others, and while rectangular in form, has generally circular depressions on the surface, recalling conditions at Far View mound before excavation. These mounds indicate large buildings in blocks, made up of many unit forms of the pure type, united into compact structures. One large dominant member of the village recalls those ruins where the village is consolidated into one community pueblo. The separation of mounds in the village and their concentration in the community house may be of chronological importance, although the relative age of the simple and composite forms can not at present be determined; but it is important to recognize that the units of construction in villages and community buildings are identical.

SUROUARO

The cluster of mounds formerly called Surouaro, now known as Yellow Jacket Spring Ruin, is situated near the head of the canyon of the same name to the left of the Monticello road, 14 miles west of Dolores. This village (pls. 1, c; 2, c) contains both large and small houses of the pure pueblo type, covering an area somewhat less than the Mummy Lake group, on the Mesa Verde. The arrangement of mounds in clusters naturally recalls the Galisteo and Jemez districts, New Mexico, where, however, the arrangement of the mounds and the structure of each is different. The individual houses in a Mesa Verde or Yellow Jacket village were not so grouped as to inclose a rectangular court, but were irregularly distributed with intervals of considerable size between them.[13]

The largest mound in the Surouaro village, shown in plate 1, c, corresponds with the so-called "Upper House" of Aztec Spring Ruin, but is much larger than Far View or any other single mound in the Mummy Lake village.

Surouaro was one of the first ruins in this region described by American explorers, attention having been first called to it by Professor Newberry,[14] whose description follows: "Surouaro is the name of a ruined town which must have once contained a population of several thousands. The name is said to be of Indian (Utah) origin, and to signify desolation, and certainly no better could have been selected.... The houses are, many of them, large, and all built of stone, hammer dressed on the exposed faces. Fragments of pottery are exceedingly common, though like the buildings, showing great age.... The remains of *metates* (corn mills) are abundant about the ruins. The ruins of several large reservoirs, built of masonry, may be seen at Surouaro, and there are traces of acequias which led to them, through which water was brought, perhaps from a great distance."

GOODMAN POINT RUIN

This ruin is a cluster of small mounds surrounding larger ones, recalling the arrangement at Aztec Spring. They naturally fall into two groups which from their direction or relation to the adjacent spring may be called the south and north sections.

The most important mound of the south section, Block A, measures 74 feet on the north, 79 feet on the south, and 76 feet on the west side. This large mound corresponds morphologically to the "Upper House" at Aztec Spring (fig. 1, A). About it there are arranged at intervals, mainly on the north and east sides, other smaller mounds generally indicating rectangular buildings. The southeast angle of the largest is connected by a low wall with one of the smaller mounds, forming an enclosure called a court, whose northern border is the rim of the canyon just above the spring. A determination of the detailed architectural features of the building buried under Block A is not possible, as none of its walls stand above the mass of fallen stones, but it is evident, from circular depressions and fragments of straight walls that appear over the surface of the mound, that the rooms were of two kinds, rectangular forms, or dwellings, and circular chambers, or kivas. This mound resembles Far View House on the Mesa Verde before excavation.

A large circular depression, 56 feet in diameter, is situated in the midst of the largest mounds. A unique feature of this depression, recognized and described by Doctor Prudden, are four piles of stones, regularly arranged on the floor. The author adopts the suggestion that this area was once roofed and served as a central circular kiva, necessitating a roof of such dimensions that four masonry pillars served for its support. The mound measures about 15 feet in height, and has large trees growing on its surface, offering evidence of a considerable age. Several other rooms are indicated by circular surface depressions, but their relation to the rectangular rooms can be determined only by excavation.

JOHNSON RUIN

This ruin, to which the author was conducted by Mr. C. K. Davis, is about 4 miles west of the Goodman Point Ruin near Mr. Johnson's ranch house, in section 12, township 36, range 18. It is said to be situated at the head of Sand Canyon, a tributary of the McElmo, and is one of the largest ruins visited. The remains of former houses skirt the rim of the canyon head for fully half a mile, forming a continuous series of mounds in which can be traced towers, great houses, and other types of buildings, and numerous depressions indicating sunken kivas. The walls of these buildings were, however, so tumbled down that little now remains above ground save piles of stones in which tops of buried walls may still be detected, but not without some difficulty. In a cave under the "mesa rim" there is a small cliff-house in the walls of which extremities of the original wooden rafters still remain in place.

In an open clearing, about 3 miles south and west of Mr. J. W. Fulk's house, Renaraye post office, there is a small ruin of rectangular form, the ground plan of which shows two rectangular sections of different sizes, joined at one angle. The largest section measures approximately 20 by 50 feet. It consists of low rooms surrounding two circular depressions, possibly kivas. Although constructed on a small scale, this section reminds one of the Upper House of Aztec Spring Ruin. The smaller section, which also has a rectangular form, has remains of high rooms on opposite sides and low walls on the remaining sides. In the enclosed area there is a circular depression or reservoir, corresponding with the reservoir of the Lower House at Aztec Spring Ruin.

BUG MESA RUIN

The author was guided by Mr. H. S. Merchant to a village ruin, one of the largest visited, situated a few miles from his ranch house. This village is about 10 miles due south of the store at the head of Dove Creek, and consists of several large mounds, each about 500 feet long, arranged parallel to each other, and numerous isolated smaller mounds. Not far from this large ruin there is a prehistoric reservoir estimated as covering about 4 acres. Many circular depressions, indicated kivas, and lines of stones showed tops of buried rectangular rooms. Excavations in a small mound near this ruin were conducted by Doctor Prudden.[15]

The canyon which heads near the corral on the road to Merchant's house revealed no evidence of prehistoric dwellings.

MITCHELL SPRING RUIN

This ruin takes its name from the earliest known description of it by Morgan,[16] which was compiled from notes by Mr. Mitchell, one of the early settlers in Montezuma Valley. Morgan's account is as follows:

"Near Mr. Mitchell's ranch, and within a space of less than a mile square, are the ruins of nine pueblo houses of moderate size. They are built of sandstone intermixed with cobblestone and adobe mortar. They are now in a very ruinous condition, without standing walls in any part of them above the rubbish. The largest of the number is marked No. 1 in the plan, figure 44, of which the outline of the original structure is still discernible. It is 94 feet in length and 47 feet in depth, and shows the remains of a stone wall in front inclosing a small court about 15 feet wide. The mass of material over some parts of this structure is 10 or 12 feet deep. There are, no doubt, rooms with a portion of the walls still standing covered with rubbish, the removal of which would reveal a considerable portion of the original ground plan."

The author paid a short visit to the Mitchell Spring village and by means of Morgan's sketch map was able to identify without difficulty the nine mounds and tower he represents. The village at Mitchell Spring differs from that at Mud Spring and at Aztec Spring mainly in the small size and diffuse distribution of the component mounds and an absence of any one mound larger than the remainder. It had, however, a round tower, but unlike that at Mud Spring village, this structure is not united to one of the houses. The addition of towers to pueblos, as pointed out by Doctor Prudden[17] several years ago, marks the highest development of pueblo architecture as shown not only in open-air villages but also in some of the large cliff pueblos, like Cliff Palace. Isolated towers are as a rule earlier in construction.

The unit type mound uncovered by Doctor Prudden is one of the most instructive examples of this type in Montezuma Canyon, but the author in subsequent pages will call attention to the existence of the same type in Square Tower Canyon. All of these pueblos probably have kivas of the pure type, practically the same in structure as Far View House on the Mesa Verde National Park.

MUD SPRING (BURKHARDT) RUIN

The collection of mounds (pl. 3, b), sometimes called Burkhardt Ruin, situated at Mud Spring, belongs to the McElmo series. This ruin, in which is the "triple-walled tower" of Holmes, for uniformity with Mitchell Spring Ruin and Aztec Spring Ruin, is named after a neighboring spring. Like these, it is a cluster of mounds forming a village which covers a considerable area. The arroyo on which it is situated opens into the McElmo, and is about 7 miles southwest from Cortez, at a point where the road enters the McElmo Canyon.

The extension of the area covered by the Mud Spring mounds is east-west, the largest mounds being those on the east. These latter are separated from the remainder, or those on the west, by a shallow, narrow gulch. There are two towers united to the western section overlooking the spring, the following description of one of which, with a sketch of the ground plan, is given by Holmes.[18]

"The circular structures or towers have been built, in the usual manner, of roughly hewn stone, and rank among the very best specimens of this ancient architecture. The great tower is especially noticeable.... In dimensions it is almost identical with the great tower of the Rio Mancos. The walls are traceable nearly all the way round, and the space between the two outer ones, which is about 5 feet in width, contains 14 apartments or cells. The walls about one of these cells are still standing to the height of 12 feet; but the interior can not be examined on account of the rubbish which fills it to the top. No openings are noticeable in the circular walls, but doorways seem to have been made to communicate between the apartments; one is preserved at d.... This tower stands back about 100 feet from the edge of the mesa near the border of the village. The smaller tower, b, stands forward on a point that overlooks the shallow gulch; it is 15 feet in diameter; the walls are 3½ feet thick and 5 feet high on the outside. Beneath this ruin, in a little side gulch, are the remains of a wall 12 feet high and 20 inches thick.... The apartments number nearly a hundred, and seem, generally, to have been rectangular. They are not, however, of uniform size, and certainly not arranged in regular order."

Morgan[19] gives the following description of the same ruin which seems to the author to be the Mud Creek village:

"Four miles westerly [from Mitchell ranch], near the ranch of Mr. Shirt, are the ruins of another large stone pueblo, together with an Indian cemetery, where each grave is marked by a border of flat stones set level with the ground in the form of a parallelogram 8 feet by 4 feet. Near the cluster of nine pueblos shown in the figure are found strewn on the ground numerous fragments of pottery of high grade in the ornamentation, and small arrowheads of flint, quartz, and chalcedony delicately formed, and small knife blades with convex and serrated edges in considerable numbers.

"This is an immense ruin with small portions of the walls still standing, particularly of the round tower of stone of three concentric walls, incorporated in the structure, and a few chambers in the north end of the main building. The round tower is still standing nearly to the height of the first story. In its present condition it was impossible to make a ground plan showing the several chambers, or to determine with certainty which side was the front of the structure, assuming that it was constructed in the terraced form.... The Round Tower is the most singular feature in this structure. While it resembles the ordinary *estufa*, common to all these structures, it differs from them in having three concentric walls. No doorways are visible in the portion still standing, consequently it must have been entered through the roof, in which respect it agrees with the ordinary *estufa*. The inner chamber is about 20 feet in diameter, and the spaces between the encircling walls are about 2 feet each; the walls are about 2 feet in thickness, and were laid up mainly with stones about 4 inches square, and, for the most part, in courses. There is a similar round tower, having but two concentric walls, at the head of the McElmo Canyon, and near the ranch of Mr. Mitchell [Mitchell Ruin]."

As the name Mud Spring is locally known to the natives, especially to employees of livery stables and garages, the ruin is here called Mud Spring. The tower and the other circular buildings are united to other rooms as in similar groups of mounds. The presence of surface depressions, thought to indicate circular kivas,[20] shows that the Mud Spring mounds are remains of a village of the same type as the Mummy Lake group, but with towers united to the largest mounds.

The time the author could give to his visit to the Mud Spring Ruin (pl. 3, *b*) was too limited to survey it, but he noticed in addition to the two circular buildings already recorded, a large mound situated on the west side of the gulch, and numerous small mounds on the east side of the same, each apparently with a central depression like a kiva. All these mounds have been more or less mutilated by indiscriminate digging, but many mounds, still untouched, remain to be excavated before we can form an adequate conception of the group. The "triple-walled tower" is now in such a condition that the author could not determine whether it was formerly circular or **D**-shaped; the "small tower" is in even worse condition and its previous form could not be made out. The Mud Spring mounds cover a much larger area than descriptions or ground plans thus far published would indicate.

Originally Mud Spring Ruin consisted of a cluster of pueblos of various sizes, each probably with a circular kiva and rectangular rooms, combined with one or more towers at present too much dilapidated to determine architectural details without excavations. Like the other clusters of pueblos in the McElmo and Montezuma Valley, the cemetery near Mud Spring Ruin has suffered considerably from pothunters, but there still remain many standing walls that are well preserved.

RUIN WITH SEMICIRCULAR CORE

This ruin is situated on the San Juan about 3 miles below the sandy bed of the mouth of the Montezuma, on a bluff 50 feet above the river. The ground plan by Jackson[21] indicates a building shaped like a trapezoid, 158 feet on the northeast side, 120 on the southeast, and 32 on the northwest side. The southwest side is broken midway by a reentering area at the rim of the bluff over the river.

In the center of this trapezoidal structure there is represented a series of rooms arranged like those of Horseshoe House, but composed of a half-circular chamber surrounded by seven rooms between two concentric circular walls. Thus far the homology to Horseshoe House is close but beyond this series of rooms, following out the trapezoidal form, at least five other rooms appear on the ground plan. The position of these recalls the walls arranged around the tower at Mud Spring village. In other words, the ruin resembles Horseshoe House, but has in addition rectangular rooms added on three sides, forming an angular building. So far as the author's information goes, no other ruin of exactly this type, which recalls Sun Temple, has been described by other observers.

WOLLEY RANCH RUIN

Wolley Ranch Ruin, situated 10 miles south of Dolores, is one of the largest mounds near Cortez. There are evidences of the former existence of a cluster of mounds at this place, only one of which now remains. This is covered with bushes, rendering it difficult to trace the bounding walls.

Blanchard Ruin

Several years ago private parties constructed at Manitou, near Colorado Springs, a cliff-dwelling on the combined plan of Spruce-tree House and Cliff Palace. The rocks used for that purpose were transported from a large mound on the Blanchard ranch near Lebanon, in the Montezuma Valley, at the head of Hartman's draw, about 6 miles south of Dolores. Two mounds (pl. 2, a, b), about three-quarters of a mile apart, are all that now remain of a considerable village; the other smaller mounds, reported by pioneer settlers, have long since been leveled by cultivation. As both of these mounds have been extensively dug into to obtain stones, the walls that remain standing show much mutilation. The present condition of the largest Blanchard mound, as seen from its southwest angle, is shown in plate 2, b. About half of the mound, now covered with a growth of bushes, still remains entire, exposing walls of fine masonry, on its south side. The rooms in the buried buildings are hard to make out on account of this covering of vegetation and accumulated débris; but the central depressions, supposed to be kivas, almost always present in the middle of mounds in this district, show that the structure of Blanchard Ruin follows the pure type.

Ruins at Aztec Spring

The mounds at Aztec Spring (pl. 1, b), situated on the eastern flank of Ute Mountain, at a site looking across the valley to the west end of Mesa Verde, were described forty years ago by W. W. Jackson[22] and Prof. W. H. Holmes.[23] The descriptions given by both these pioneers are quoted at length for the reason that subsequent authors have added little from direct observation since that time, notwithstanding they have been constantly referred to and the illustrations reproduced.

As a result of a short visit, the author is able to add the few following notes on the Aztec Spring mounds. The ruin is a village consisting of a cluster of unit pueblos of the pure type in various stages of consolidation. No excavations were made, but the surface indications point to the conclusion that the different mounds indicate that these pueblos have different shapes and sizes.

The author's observations differ in several unimportant particulars from those of previous writers, and while it is not his intention to describe in detail the Aztec Spring village he will call attention to certain features it shares with other villages in the Montezuma Valley.

The best, almost the only accounts of this village are the following taken from the descriptions by Jackson and Holmes published in 1877. Mr. Jackson gives the following description:[24]

"Immediately adjoining the spring, on the right, as we face it from below, is the ruin of a great massive structure [Upper House?] of some kind, about 100 feet square in exterior dimensions; a portion only of the wall upon the northern face remaining in its original position. The *débris* of the ruin now forms a great mound of crumbling rock, from 12 to 20 feet in height, overgrown with artemisia, but showing clearly, however, its rectangular structure, adjusted approximately to the four points of the compass. Inside this square is a circle, about 60 feet in diameter, deeply depressed in the center. The space between the square and the circle appeared, upon a hasty examination, to have been filled in solidly with a sort of rubble-masonry. Cross-walls were noticed in two places; but whether they were to strengthen the walls or divided apartments could only be conjectured. That portion of the outer wall remaining standing is some 40 feet in length and 15 in height. The stones were dressed to a uniform size and finish. Upon the same level as this ruin, and extending back some distance, were grouped line after line of foundations and mounds, the great mass of which is of stone but not one remaining upon another.... Below the above group, some 200 yards distant, and communicating by indistinct lines of *débris*, is another great wall, inclosing a space of about 200 feet square [Lower House?].... This better preserved portion is some 50 feet in length, 7 or 8 feet in height, and 20 feet thick, the two exterior surfaces of well-dressed and evenly laid courses, and the center packed in solidly with rubble-masonry, looking entirely different from those rooms which had been filled with *débris*, though it is difficult to assign any reason for its being so massively constructed.... The town built about this spring is nearly a square mile in extent, the larger and more enduring buildings in the center, while all about are scattered and grouped the remnants of smaller structures, comprising the suburbs."

The description by Professor Holmes[25] is more detailed and accompanied by a ground plan, and is quoted below:

"The site of the spring I found, but without the least appearance of water. The depression formerly occupied by it is near the center of a large mass of ruins, similar to the group [Mud Spring village] last described, but having a rectangular instead of a circular building as the chief and central structure. This I have called the *upper house* in the plate, and a large walled enclosure a little lower on the slope I have for the sake of distinction called the *lower house*.

"These ruins form the most imposing pile of masonry yet [1875] found in Colorado. The whole group covers an area about 480,000 square feet, and has an average depth of from 3 to 4 feet. This would give in the vicinity of 1,500,000 solid feet of stonework. The stone used is chiefly of the fossiliferous limestone that outcrop along the base of the Mesa Verde a mile or more away, and its transportation to this place has doubtless been a great work for a people so totally without facilities.

"The upper house is rectangular, measuring 80 feet by 100 feet, and is built with the cardinal points to within a few degrees. The pile is from 12 to 15 feet in height, and its massiveness suggests an original height at least twice as great. The plan is somewhat difficult to make out on account of the very great quantity of *débris*.

"The walls seem to have been double, with a space 7 feet between; a number of cross-walls at regular intervals indicate that this space has been divided into apartments, as seen in the plan.

"The walls are 26 inches thick, and are built of roughly dressed stones, which were probably laid in mortar, as in other cases.

"The enclosed space, which is somewhat depressed, has two lines of *débris*, probably the remains of partition-walls, separating it into three apartments, *a, b, c* [note]. Enclosing this great house is a network of fallen walls, so completely reduced that none of the stones seem to remain in place; and I am at a loss to determine whether they mark the site of a cluster of irregular apartments, having low, loosely built walls, or whether they are the remains of some imposing adobe structure built after the manner of the ruined pueblos of the Rio Chaco.

"Two well-defined circular enclosures or *estufas* [kivas] are situated in the midst of the southern wing of the ruin. The upper one, A, is on the opposite side of the spring from the great house, is 60 feet in diameter, and is surrounded by a low stone wall. West of the house is a small open court, which seems to have had a gateway opening out to the west, through the surrounding walls.

"The lower house is 200 feet in length by 180 in width, and its walls vary 15 degrees from the cardinal points. The northern wall, *a*, is double and contains a row of eight apartments about 7 feet in width by 24 in length. The walls of the other sides are low, and seem to have served simply to enclose the great court, near the center of which is a large walled depression (*estufa* B)."

The number of buildings that composed the Aztec Spring village ([fig. 1](#)) when it was inhabited can not be exactly estimated, but as indicated by the largest mound, the most important block of rooms exceeds in size any at Mitchell Spring Ruin. While this village also covered more ground than that at Mud Spring, it shows no evidence of added towers, a prominent feature of the largest mound of the latter. Two sections ([fig. 1, *A, B*](#)) may be distinguished in the arrangement of mounds in the village; one may be known as the western and the other as the eastern division.

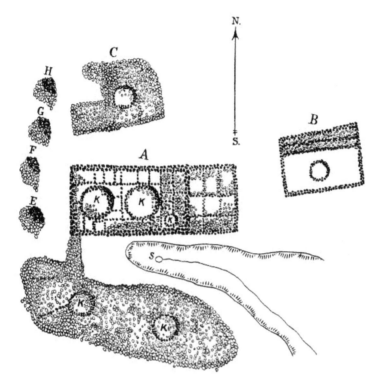

FIG. 1.—Ground plan of Aztec Spring Ruin.

The highest and most conspicuous mound of the western section (*A*) is referred to by Professor Holmes as the "Upper House." Surface characteristics now indicate that this is the remains of a compact rectangular building, with circular kivas and domiciliary rooms of different shapes, the arrangement of which can not be determined without extensive excavations. The plan of this pueblo published by Holmes[26] shows two large and one small depression, indicating peripheral rectangular chambers surrounded by walls of rectangular rooms.

The author interprets the depressions, *K*, as kivas, but supposes that they were not rectangular as figured by Holmes, but circular, surrounded on all four sides by square secular chambers, the "Upper House" being formed by the consolidation of several units of the pure pueblo type. Although Aztec Spring Ruin is now much mutilated and its walls difficult to trace, the surface indications, aided by comparative studies of the rooms, show that Holmes' "*a*," "*b*," and "*c*," now shown by depressions, are circular, subterranean kivas. They are the same kind of chambers as the circular depressions in the mounds on the south side of the spring. The height of the mound called "Upper House" indicates that the building had more than one story on the west and north sides, and that a series of rooms one story high with accompanying circular depressions existed on the east side.

The "Upper House" is only one of several pueblos composing the western cluster of the Aztec Spring village. Its proximity to the source of water may in part account for its predominant size, but there are evidences of several other mounds (*E-H*) in its neighborhood, also remains of pueblos. Those on the north (*C*) and west sides (*E-H*) are small and separated from it by intervals sometimes called courts. The most extensive accumulation of rooms next the "Upper House" is situated across the draw in which the spring lies, south of the "Upper House" cluster already considered. The aggregation of houses near the "Upper House" is mainly composed of low rectangular buildings among which are recognized scattered circular depressions indicating kivas. The largest of these buildings is indicated by the mound on the south rim of the draw, where we can make out remains of a number of circular depressions or kivas (*K*), as if several unit forms fused together; on the north and west sides of the spring there are small, low mounds, unconnected, also suggesting several similar unit forms. The most densely populated part of the village at Aztec Spring, as indicated by the size of the mounds clustered on the rim around the head of the draw, is above the spring, on the northwest and south sides.

There remains to be mentioned the eastern annex (*B*) of the Aztec Spring village, the most striking remains of which is a rectangular inclosure called "Lower House," situated east of the spring and lower down the draw, or at a lower level than the section already considered. The type of this structure, which undoubtedly belonged to the same village, is different from that already described. It resembles a reservoir rather than a kiva, inclosed by a low rectangular wall, with rows of rooms on the north side. The court of the "Lower House" measures 218 feet. The wall on the east, south, and west sides is only a few feet high and is narrow; that on the north is broader and higher, evidently the remains of rooms, overlooking the inclosed area.

Perhaps the most enigmatical structures in the vicinity of Aztec Spring village are situated on a low mesa south of the mounds, a few hundred feet away. These are circular depressions without accompanying mounds, one of which was excavated a few years ago to the depth of 12 feet; on the south there was discovered a well-made wall of a circular opening, now visible, by which there was a communication through a horizontal tunnel with the open air. The author was informed that this tunnel is artificial and that one of the workmen crawled through it to its opening in the side of a bank many yards distant.

No attempt was made to get the exact dimensions of the component houses at Aztec Spring, as the walls are now concealed in the mounds, and measurements can only be approximations if obtained from surface indications without excavation. The sketch plan here introduced (fig. 1) is schematic, but although not claimed as accurate, may serve to convey a better idea of the relation of the two great structures and their annexed buildings than any previously advanced.

The author saw no ruined prehistoric village in the Montezuma Valley that so stirred his enthusiasm to properly excavate and repair as that at Aztec Spring,[27] notwithstanding it has been considerably dug over for commercial purposes.

GREAT OPEN-AIR RUINS SOUTH AND SOUTHWEST OF DOVE CREEK POST OFFICE

In the region south and southwest of Dove Creek there are several large pueblo ruins, indicated by mounds formed of trimmed stone, eolean sand, and clay from plastering, which have certain characters in common. Each mound is a large heap of stones (pl. 3, a) near which is a depression or reservoir, with smaller heaps which in different ruins show the small buildings of the unit type. These clusters or villages are somewhat modified in form by the configuration of the mesa surface. The larger have rectangular forms regularly disposed in blocks with passageways between them or are without any definite arrangement.

SQUAW POINT RUIN

This large ruin, which has been described by Doctor Prudden as Squaw Point Ruin and as Pierson Lake Ruin, was visited by the author, who has little to add to this description. One of the small heaps of stone or mounds has been excavated and its structure found to conform with the definition of the unit type. The subterranean communication between one of the rectangular rooms and the kiva could be well seen at the time of the author's visit and recalls the feature pointed out by him in some of the kivas of Spruce-tree House. The large reservoir and the great ruin are noteworthy features of the Squaw Point settlement.

It seems to the author that the large block of buildings is simply a congeries of unit types the structure of one of which is indicated by the small buildings excavated by Doctor Prudden, and that structurally there is the same condition in it as in the pueblo ruins of Montezuma Valley, a conclusion to which the several artifacts mentioned and figured by Doctor Prudden also point.

The same holds true of Bug Point Ruin, a few miles away, also excavated and described by Doctor Prudden. Here also excavation of a small mound shows the unit type, and while no one has yet opened the larger mound or pueblo, superficial evidences indicate that it also is a complex of many unit types joined together. Until more facts are available the relative age of the small unit types as compared to the large pueblo can not be definitely stated, but there is little reason to doubt that they are contemporaneous, and nothing to support the belief that they do not indicate the same culture.

ACMEN RUIN

Following the Old Bluff Road and leaving it about 5 miles west of Acmen post office, one comes to a low canyon beyond Pigge ranch. The heaps of stone or large mounds cover an area of about 10 acres, the largest being about 15 feet high. East of this is a circular depression surrounded by stones, indicating either a reservoir or a ruined building.

The top of the highest mound (pl. 3, a)—no walls stand above the surface—is depressed like mounds of the Mummy Lake group on the Mesa Verde. This depression probably indicates a circular kiva embedded in square walls, the masonry of which so far as can be judged superficially is not very fine. There are many smaller mounds in the vicinity and evidences of cemeteries on the south, east, and west sides, where there are evidences of desultory digging; fragments of pottery are numerous.

These mounds indicate a considerable village which would well repay excavation, as shown by the numerous specimens of corrugated, black and white, and red pottery in the Pigge collection, made in a small mound near the Pigge ranch.

The specimens in this collection present few features different from those indicated by the fragments of pottery picked up on the larger mounds a mile west of the site where they were excavated. They are the same as shards from the mounds in the McElmo region.

OAK SPRING HOUSE

About 15 miles southwest of Dove Creek on Monument Canyon there is a good spring called Oak Spring, near which are several piles of stones indicating former buildings, the largest of which, about a quarter of a mile away, has a central depression with surrounding walls now covered with rock or buried in soil or blown sand. Very large piñon trees grow on top of the highest walls of this ruin, the general features of which recall those at Bug Spring, though their size is considerably less. In the surface of rock above the spring there are numerous potholes of small size. One of these, 4 feet deep and about 18 feet in diameter, is almost perfectly circular and has some signs of having been deepened artificially. It holds water much of the time and was undoubtedly a source of water supply to the aborigines, as it now is to stock in that neighborhood.

RUIN IN RUIN CANYON

One of the large rim-rock ruins may be seen on the left bank of Ruin Canyon in full view from the Old Bluff Road. The ruin is an immense pile of stones perched on the very edge of the rim, with no walls standing above the surface. The most striking feature of this ruin is the cliff-house below, the walls and entrance into which are visible from the road (pl. 9, b). It is readily accessible and one of the largest in the country. On either side of the Old Bluff Road from Ruin Canyon to the "Aztec Reservoir" small piles of stone mark the sites of many former buildings of the one-house type which can readily be seen, especially in the sagebrush clearings as the road descends to the Picket corral, the reservoirs, and the McElmo Canyon.

CANNONBALL RUIN

One of the most instructive ruins of the McElmo Canyon region is situated at the head of Cannonball Canyon, a short distance across the mesa north of the McElmo, at a point nearly opposite the store. This ruin is made up of two separate pueblos facing each other, one of which is known as the northern, the other as the southern pueblo (pl. 22, b). Both show castellated chambers and towers, one of which is situated at the bottom of the canyon. The southern pueblo was excavated a few years ago by Mr. S. G. Morley, who published an excellent plan and a good description of it, and made several suggestions regarding additions of new rooms to the kivas which are valuable. Its walls were not protected and are rapidly deteriorating.

This pueblo, as pointed out by Mr. Morley,[28] has 29 secular rooms arranged with little regularity, and 7 circular kivas, belonging to the vaulted-roofed variety. It is a fine example of a composite pueblo of the pure type, in which there are several large kivas. Morley has pointed out a possible sequence in the addition of the different kivas to a preexisting tower and offers an explanation of the chronological steps by which he thinks the aggregation of rooms was brought about. Occasionally we find inserted in the walls of these houses large artificially worked or uncut flat stones, such as the author has mentioned as existing in the walls of the northwest corner of the court of Far View House. This Cyclopean form of masonry is primitive and may be looked upon as a survival of a ruder and more archaic condition best shown in the Montezuma Mesa ruins farther west, a good example of which was described by Jackson.[29]

CIRCULAR RUINS WITH PERIPHERAL COMPARTMENTS

It has long been recognized that circular ruins in the Southwest differ from rectangular ruins, not only in shape but also in structural features, as relative position and character of kivas. The relation of the ceremonial chambers to the houses, no less than the external forms of the two, at first sight appear to separate them from the pure type.[30] They are more numerous and probably more ancient, as their relative abundance implies.

These circular ruins, in which group is included certain modifications where the curve of one side is replaced (generally on the south) by a straight wall or chord, have several concentric walls; again, they take the form of simple towers with one row of encircling compartments, or they may have a double wall with inclosed compartments.

Many representations of semicircular ruins were found in the region here considered, some of which are of considerable size. The simplest form is well illustrated by the **D**-shaped building, Horseshoe House, in Hackberry Canyon, a ruin which will be considered later in this article. Other examples occur in the Yellow Jacket, and there are several, as Butte Ruin, Emerson, and Escalante Ruins, in the neighborhood of Dolores.

In contrast to the village type consisting of a number of pueblos clustered together, but separated from each other, where the growth takes place mainly through the union of components, the circular ruin in enlarging its size apparently did so by the addition of new compartments peripherally or like additional rings in exogenous trees. Judging from their frequency, the center of distribution of the circular type lies somewhere in the San Juan culture area. This type does not occur in the Gila Valley or its tributaries, where we have an architectural zone denoting that a people somewhat different in culture from the Pueblos exists, but occurs throughout the "Central Zone," so called, extending across New Mexico from Colorado as far south as Zuñi. Many additional observations remain to be made before we can adequately define the group known as the circular type and the extent of the area over which it is distributed.

The following examples of this type have been studied by the author:

WOOD CANYON RUINS

Reports were brought to the author of large ruins on the rim of Wood Canyon, about 4 miles south of Yellow Jacket post office, in October, 1918, when he had almost finished the season's work. Two ruins of size were examined, one of which, situated in the open sagebrush clearing, belongs to the village type composed of large and small rectangular mounds. The other is composed of small circular or semicircular buildings with a surrounding wall. The form of this latter (fig. 2) would seem to place it in a subgroup or village type. Approach to the inclosed circular mounds was debarred by a high bluff of a canyon on one side and by a low defensive curved wall (E), some of the stones of which are large, almost megaliths, on the side of the mesa. From fragmentary sections of the buried walls of one of these circular mounds (A, B), which appear on the surface, it would seem that the buildings were like towers (C, D). This is one of the few known examples of circular buildings in an area protected by a curved wall. In the cliffs below Wood Canyon Ruin is a cliff-dwelling (G, H, J) remarkable mainly in its site.

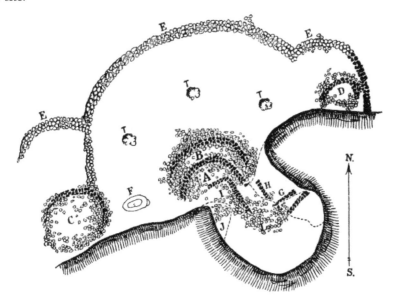

FIG. 2.—Ground plan of Wood Canyon Ruin.

BUTTE RUIN

The so-called Butte Ruin, situated in Lost Canyon, 5 miles east of Dolores, belongs to the circular type. It crowns a low elevation, steep on the west side, sloping more gradually on the east, and surrounded by cultivated fields. The view from its top looking toward Ute Mountain and the Mesa Verde plateau is particularly extensive. The butte is forested by a few spruces growing at the base and extending up the sides, which are replaced at the summit by a thick growth of sage and other bushes which cover the mound, rendering it difficult to make out the ground plan of the ruin on its top.

From what appears on the surface it would seem that this ruin was a circular or semicircular building about 60 feet in diameter, the walls rising about 10 feet high. Like other circular mounds it shows a well-marked depression in the middle, from which radiate walls or indications of walled compartments. Like the majority of the buildings of the circular form, the walls on one side have fallen, suggesting that a low straight wall, possibly with rectangular rooms, was annexed to this side.

In the neighborhood of Butte Ruin there is another hill crowned with a pile of stones, probably a round building of smaller size and with more dilapidated walls. Old cedar beams project in places out of the mounds.

The cliff-houses below the largest of these mounds show well-made walls with a few rafters and beams. There are pictographs on the cliff a short distance away.

EMERSON RUIN

This ruin crowns a low hill about 3 miles south of Dolores (fig. 3). The form of the mound is semicircular with a depression in the middle around which can be traced radiating partitions suggesting compartments. Its outer wall on the south side, as in so many other examples of this type, has fallen, and the indications are that here the wall was straight, or like that on the south side of Horseshoe Ruin.

The author's attention was first called to this ruin by Mr. Gordon Parker, supervisor of the Montezuma Forest Reserve, it having been discovered by Mr. J. W. Emerson, one of his rangers. The circular or semicircular form (fig. 4) of the mound indicates at once that it does not belong to the same type as Far View House; the central depression is surrounded by a series of compartments separated by radiating walls like the circular ruins in the pueblo region to the south. Mr. Emerson's report, which follows, points out the main features of this remarkable ruin.[31]

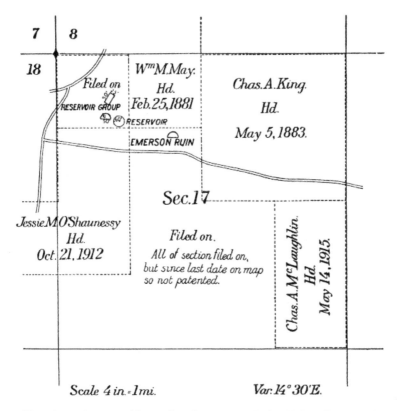

FIG. 3.—Metes and bounds of Emerson Ruin. (After Emerson.)

DOLORES, COLORADO, *July 7, 1917.*

In August, 1916, I visited Mesa Verde National Park. While there Doctor Fewkes inquired in regard to ruins in the vicinity of the Big Bend of the Dolores River. He informed me that the log of two old Spanish explorers of 1775 described a ruin near the bend of the Dolores River as of great value.

Later, during October, 1916, I visited a number of ruins in this vicinity, including the one which (for the want of a better name) I have mapped and named Sun Dial Palace. Later, last fall, I again visited these ruins with Mr. R. W. Williamson, of Dolores, Colorado.

On July 5, 1917, I again visited these ruins, which I have designated as Reservoir Group and Sun Dial Palace.[32] For location and status of land on which they lie see map of sec. 17, T. 37 N., R. 15 W., N. M. P. M. (fig. 3).

While examining Sun Dial Palace I noted the "**D**-shaped construction, also that the south wall of the building ran due east and west." Also please note the regularity of wall bearings from the approximate center of the elliptical center chamber. I also noted that a shadow cast by the sun apparently coincides with some of these walls at different hours during the day. This last gave suggestion to the name. Also please note that the first tier of rooms around the middle chamber does not show a complete set of bearings but seems to suggest that these regular bearings were obtained from observation and study of a master builder. The result of his study was built as the next circular room tier was added. The two missing rooms on the western side of the building seem to suggest that this building was never completed, and also bear out my theory of an outward building of room tiers from the middle chamber.

On the ground this building is fully completed on the south side and forms a due east and west line. An error in mapping the elliptical middle chamber has given the south side an incomplete appearance.

I believe that the excavation and study of this ruin will recall something of value, as Father Escalante wrote in his log in 1775.

Respectfully submitted.

(Signed) J. WARD EMERSON,
Forest Ranger.

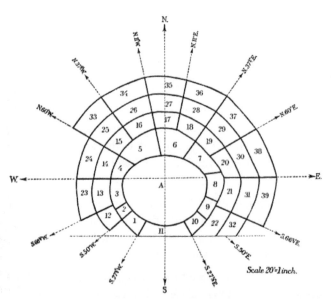

FIG. 4.—Schematic ground plan of Emerson Ruin. (After Emerson.)

A personal examination of the remains of this building leads the author to the conclusion that while it belongs to the circular group, with a ground plan resembling Horseshoe House, and while the central part had a wall completely circular, the outer concentric curved walls did not complete their course on the south side, but ended in straight walls comparable with the partitions separating compartments. The author identifies another ruin as that mentioned by the Catholic fathers in 1775.

ESCALANTE RUIN

The name Escalante Ruin, given to the first ruin recorded by a white man in Colorado, is situated about 3 miles from Dolores on top of a low hill to the right of the Monticello Road, just beyond where it diverges from the road to Cortez. The outline of the pile of stones suggests a **D**-shaped or semicircular house with a central depression surrounded by rooms separated by radiating partitions. The wall on the south or east sides was probably straight, rendering the form not greatly unlike the other ruins on hilltops in the neighborhood of Dolores.

This is supposed to be the ruin to which reference is made in the following quotation from an article in Science:[33]

"There is in the Congressional Library, among the documents collected by Peter Force, a manuscript diary of early exploration in New Mexico, Colorado, and Utah, dated 1776, written by two Catholic priests, Father Silvester Velez Escalante and Father Francisco Atanacio Dominguez. This diary is valuable to students of archeology, as it contains the first reference to a prehistoric ruin in the confines of the present State of Colorado, although the mention is too brief for positive identification of the ruin.[34] While the context indicates its approximate site, there are at this place at least two large ruins, either of which might be that referred to. I have no doubt which one of these two ruins was indicated by these early explorers, but my interest in this ruin is both archeological and historical. Our knowledge of the structure of these ruins is at the present day almost as imperfect as it was a century and a half ago.

"The route followed by the writers of the diary was possibly an Indian pathway, and is now called the Old Spanish Trail. After entering Colorado it ran from near the present site of Mancos to the Dolores. On the fourteenth day from Santa Fe, we find the following entry: 'En la vanda austral del Vio [Rio] sobre un alto, huvo anti-quam (te) una Poblacion pequeña, de la misma forma q☐ las de los Indios el Nuevo Mexico, segun manifieran las Ruinas q☐ de invento registramos.'

"By tracing the trip day by day, up to that time, it appears that the ruin referred to by these early fathers was situated somewhere near the bend of the Dolores River, or not far from the present town Dolores, Colo. The above quotation indicates that the ruin was a small settlement, and situated on a hill, on the south side of the river or trail, but it did not differ greatly from the ruined settlements of the Indians of New Mexico with which the writers were familiar, and had already described."

CLIFF-DWELLINGS

There are numerous cliff-houses in this district, but while, as a rule, they are much smaller than the magnificent examples in the Mesa Verde, they are built on the same architectural lines as their more pretentious relatives. Both large and small have circular subterranean kivas, similarly constructed to those of Spruce-tree House, and have mural pilasters (to support a vaulted roof, now destroyed), ventilators, and deflectors.

There are also many rooms in cliffs, possibly used for storage or for some other unknown purposes, but too small for habitations. It is significant that these are identical so far as their size is concerned with the "ledge houses," near Spruce-tree House, indicating similar or identical uses.

The kivas of cliff-dwellings of size in the region considered have the same structural features as those of adjacent ruins, but very little resemblance, save in site, to those of cliff-dwellings in southern Arizona, as in the Sierra Ancha or Verde Valley, the structure of which resembles adjacent pueblos.

The absence in the McElmo region of very large cliff-houses is due partly but not wholly to geological conditions, the immense caves of the Mesa Verde not being duplicated in the tributaries of the McElmo; but wherever caverns do occur, as in Sand Canyon, we commonly find diminutive representatives. While differences in geological features may account for the size of these prehistoric buildings, the nature of the site or its size is not all important.[35]

Here and there one sees from the road through the McElmo Canyon a few small cliff-houses, and if he penetrates some of the tributaries, he finds many others. The canyon is dominated by the Ute Mountain on the south, but on the north are numerous eroded cliffs in which are many caves affording good opportunities for the construction of cliff-houses.

These buildings do not differ save in size from the cliff-houses of the Mesa Verde. Their kivas resemble the vaulted variety and the masonry is identical.

Although the existence of cliff-dwellings in the tributaries of the McElmo has long been known, the characteristic circular kivas which occur in the Mesa Verde had not been recognized previous to the present report.

The relative age of the pueblos and great towers and the same structures in caves can not be decided by the data at hand, but the indications are that they were contemporary.

On account of the similarity in structure of the McElmo cliff-dwellings to those on Mesa Verde, only a few examples from the former region are here considered. It may be worthy of note that while McElmo cliff-dwellings are generally accompanied by large open-air pueblos and towers or great houses on the cliffs above, in the Mesa Verde open-air buildings[36] are generally situated some distance from the cliff-dwellings.

CLIFF-DWELLINGS IN SAND CANYON

Several small cliff-houses occur in Sand Canyon, one of the northern tributaries of the McElmo. Stone Arch House, here figured (pl. 6, a), so-called from the eroded cliff (pl. 4, b) near by. It is situated in the cliff, about a mile from where the canyon enters the McElmo Canyon near Battle Rock. Abundant piñon trees and a few scrubby cedars grow in the low mounds of the talus below the ruin, near which, on top of a neighboring rock pinnacle, still stand the well-constructed walls of a small house (pl. 4, a).

DOUBLE CLIFF-HOUSE

The formerly unnamed cliff-house shown in plate 8[37] is one of the best preserved in Sand Canyon. It consists of an upper and a lower house, the former situated far back in the cave, the latter on a projecting terrace below. Unfortunately it is impossible to introduce an extended description of this building as it was not entered by the author's party, but from a distance the walls exhibit fine masonry. It is unique in having double buildings on different levels, an arrangement not rare in a few examples of cliff-dwellings on the Mesa Verde. As shown in plate 8, the character of the rock on which the lower house stands is harder than that above in which the cave has been eroded. The upper house is wholly protected by the roof[38] of the cave and occupies its entire floor. The lower house shows from a distance at least two rooms, the front wall of one having fallen.

From a distance the walls of both the lower and the upper house seem to be well preserved, although many of the component stones have fallen to the base of the cliff.

SCAFFOLD IN SAND CANYON

One of the cliffs bordering Sand Canyon has an inaccessible cave in which is an artificial platform or lookout shown in plate 7, a. Although this structure is not as well preserved as the scaffold in the neighborhood of Scaffold House in Laguna (Sosi) Canyon, on the Navaho National

Monument, it seems to have had a similar purpose. It is constructed of logs reaching from one side of the cave to the other supporting a floor of flat stones and adobe. Its elevated situation would necessitate for entrance either holes cut in the cliffs or ladders.

UNIT TYPE HOUSES IN CAVES

In subsequent pages the author will describe a ruin called the Unit type House, situated in the open on the north rim of Square Tower Canyon. A similar type of unit type house is found in a cave in Sand Canyon. The reader's attention may first be called to the definition of a unit type, which is a building composed of a circular kiva, with mural banquettes and pedestals supporting a vaulted roof, with ventilator, reflector, and generally a ceremonial opening near a central fire hole in the floor. This kiva (fig. 5) is generally embedded in or surrounded by rectangular rooms. The single-unit type has one kiva with several surrounding rooms; the so-called pure type is composed of these units united.

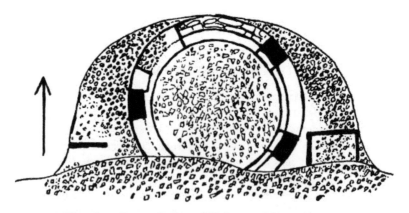

FIG. 5.—Ground plan of Unit type House in cave.

In an almost inaccessible cave (pl. 5, b) in Sand Canyon a few miles from the McElmo road near the scaffold already mentioned there is a cliff ruin, so far as known the first described single-unit house in a cave. It covers the whole floor of the cave (fig. 5) and its walls are considerably dilapidated, but the kiva shows this instructive condition: The walls are double, one inside the other, with two sets of pedestals, the outer of which are very much blackened with smoke of constant fires; the inner fresh and untarnished, evidently of late construction. A similar double-walled kiva known as "Kiva A" exists in Spruce-tree House, as described in the author's account of that ruin.[39] On the perpendicular wall of the precipice at the right hand of the ruin in the cave above mentioned are several pictographs shown in plate 7, c.

The rectangular rooms about the kiva are in places excavated out of the cliffs, but show standing walls on the front. These were not, however, constructed with the same care as those of the kiva.

The cliff-house in Hackberry Canyon (pl. 9, a) is one of the most instructive. It lies below Horseshoe House and appears to be a second example of a unit type kiva and surrounding rooms.

The cliff-dwelling in Ruin Canyon[40] visible across the canyon from the Old Bluff City Road is well preserved. On the rim of the canyon are piles of stone indicating a very large pueblo, with surface circular depressions indicating unit type houses.

CLIFF-HOUSES IN LOST CANYON

Lost Canyon, a southern tributary of the Dolores River, contains instructive cliff-houses to which my attention was called by Mr. Gordon Parker, superintendent of the Montezuma Forest Reserve, who has kindly allowed me to use the accompanying photographs. This cliff-house (pl. 10, a, b) belongs to the true Mesa Verde type and shows comparatively good preservation of its walls, some of the beams being in place. It is most easily approached from Mancos.

There are small cliff-houses in the same canyon not far from Dolores, but these are smaller and their walls very poorly preserved.

An interesting feature of these cliff-houses in Lost Canyon is that they mark the northern horizon of cliff-dwellings of the Mesa Verde type, having kivas similarly constructed.

Great Houses and Towers

Great houses and towers differ from pueblos of the pure type but may often be combined with them, forming composite houses arranged in clusters called villages. Castles and towers may be isolated structures without additional chambers, or may have many annexed rooms which are rectangular, round, or semicircular in form. Semicircular towers surrounded by concentric curved walls connected by radial partitions forming compartments are shown in Horseshoe Ruin, to which attention has been called in preceding pages, and possibly in the circular or semicircular ruins on hilltops near Dolores.

MASONRY

The masonry of the great house and tower type (pl. 11, a, b) varies in excellence, not only in different examples but also in different portions of the same building. Some of the walls contain some of the best-constructed masonry north of Mexico; others (see pl. 6, b) are crudely made. In the

Great House of the Holly group, where the walls show superior construction, the lowest courses of rock are larger than those above, but in Hovenweep Castle small stones are found below those of larger size; the Round Tower in McLean Basin shows small and large stones introduced for ornamentation.

The ambitious constructors of several towers have built the foundations of these towers on bowlders sloping at a considerable angle, and it is a source of wonder that these walls have stood for so many years without sliding from their bases. Although so well constructed in many instances, the courses were weak from their want of binding to the remaining wall. As a consequence many corners have fallen, leaving the remaining walls intact. The builders often failed to tie in the partitions to the outer walls, by which failure they lost a brace and have sprung away from their attachment.

In a general way we may recognize masonry of two varieties.

1. That in which horizontal courses are obscure or absent. This has resulted from the use of stones of different sizes, the intervals between which are filled in with masses of adobe. These stones are little fashioned, or dressed only on one side, that forming the face of the wall.

2. That constructed of horizontal courses, constituting by far the larger number of these buildings. Each course of this masonry is made of well-dressed stones, carefully pecked, and of the same size. In this horizontal masonry the thickness of stones used may vary in different courses (pl. 11, *b*). They may be alternately narrow or thick, or layers of thick stones may be separated by one or more layers of tabular or thin stones. This method of alternation may be so regular as to please the eye and thus become decorative, a mode of decoration that reached a high development in the Chaco Ruins. The stones in the horizontal style of masonry are equal in size throughout the whole building in some cases, and show not only care in choice of stones but also in dressing them to the same regulation size. In these cases the joints fit so accurately that chinking has not been found necessary and a minimum use of adobe was required.

The inner walls of kivas are much better constructed than the outer walls of the same or of the walls about them. The masonry here is regular horizontal. The sides, lintels, and thresholds of doorways are among the finest examples of construction. With the exception of walls sheltered by overhanging cliffs, the plastering has completely disappeared, but there is no reason to doubt that the interiors of all the great houses and towers were formerly plastered.

It is instructive to compare the masonry of the great houses and towers of the Mancos with that of the towers in Hill Canyon (pl. 11, c) in Utah, the most northern extension of these two types. In Eight Mile Ruin, one of the largest of these buildings in Hill Canyon, we have a circular tower with annexed great houses, all constructed of well-dressed stones, the masonry in the walls showing on one side of the tower. No excavations, however, have yet been undertaken in Hill Canyon Ruins, and it is not known whether the unit type of kiva is found there, but the combination of great houses and towers is evident from the ground plans elsewhere published.[41]

The feature of the towers in Hill Canyon is the clustering into groups, somewhat recalling the condition in Cannonball Ruin, where, however, they are united. In the Eight Mile Ruin one of the towers is separated from the remaining houses.

Several towers have accompanying circular depressions with surrounding mounds. This association can well be seen in Holmes Tower on the Mancos Canyon and in Davis Tower and one or two others on the Yellow Jacket. These depressions, sometimes called reservoirs, have never been excavated, but from what is known of rooms accompanying towers in the western section of Hovenweep Castle it may be that they indicate kivas. Some towers have no sunken area in the immediate vicinity, especially those mounted on rocky points or perched on bowlders. At Cannonball Ruin there are several kivas side by side in one section and towering above them is a massive walled tower and other rooms.

STRUCTURE OF TOWERS

None of the towers examined have evidences of mural pilasters to support a roof or recesses in the walls as in vaulted-roofed kivas. They are sometimes two stories high, the rafters and flooring resting on ledges of the inner wall. Lateral entrances are common and windows are absent.[42]

While the author has found no ruin of the same ground plan as Sun Temple on the Mesa Verde, **D**-shaped towers or great houses from several localities distantly recall this mysterious building, and there may be an identity in use between Sun Temple and the massive walled structures of the McElmo and Yellow Jacket; what that use was has not thus far been determined.[43] If they were constructed for observatories we can not account for the square tower in the South Fork of Square Tower Canyon, from which one can not even look down the canyon, much less in other directions, hemmed in as it is by cliffs. Isolated towers are often too small for defense; and they show no signs of habitation.

Are they granaries for storage of corn or places for rites and ceremonies? Do they combine several functions—observation, defense, and storage of food? Thus far in studies of more than 30 towers and great houses not one has been found so well preserved that enough remains to determine its use, and yet their walls are among the best in all southwestern ruins. Some future archeologist may find objects in towers that will demonstrate their function, but from our present knowledge no theory of their use yet suggested is satisfactory.

It is impossible from the data available to determine the century in which the towers and great houses of the region were constructed. Thus far a few were seen with great trees growing in them, but none with roofs; the state of preservation of the walls does not point to a great age. Several writers have regarded them as occupied subsequently to the Spanish conquest, while others have ascribed to them a very remote antiquity. It can hardly be questioned that the cliff-dwellers, and by inference their kindred, the tower builders, were superior in their arts to modern Pueblos.

It is important to determine first of all the forms of these towers; whether their ground plans are circular, oval, square, rectangular, or semicircular. The northern wall of many is uniformly curved and the last to fall, which might lead to the belief that the southern side, generally straight, was poorly made, but one can not determine that by direct observation, since the latter has fallen. As a matter of fact the south wall was generally low and straight, over 50 per cent of the "round" towers being semicircular, **D**-shaped, or some modification of that form; but we also have square and rectangular towers. It is also important to determine whether these had single or multiple chambers and the arrangement of the rooms in relation to them. This is especially desirable in towers with concentric compartments.

It is also instructive to know more of the association of towers with pueblos and cliff-dwellings or to analyze component architectural features. The tower type often occurs without appended rooms. At Cliff Palace and Square Tower House it is united with a pueblo village under cliffs; in Mud Spring Ruin it has a like relation to rooms of a pueblo in the open. Has its function changed by that union? What use did the tower serve when isolated and had it the same use when united with other kinds of rooms in cliff-dwellings and pueblos?

No writer on the prehistoric towers of Colorado and Utah has emphasized the fact that a large number of these buildings are semicircular or **D**-shaped, but it has been taken for granted that the fallen wall on the south side was curved, rendering the tower circular or oval.[44] In most cases this wall was the straight side of a **D**-shaped tower. Doctor Prudden, who first recognized the importance of a union of towers with other types of architecture in the McElmo district, says:[45] "Towers of various forms and heights occasionally form a part of composite ruins of various types." He says also: "Several of the houses are modified by the introduction of a round tower." And again: "At the head of a short canyon north of the Alkali, which I have called Jackson Canyon ... each building consists of an irregular mass of rooms about 200 feet long, with low towers among them."

As our studies are morphological, dealing with forms rather than sites of towers, little attention need be paid to their situation on bowlders, in cliffs, or at the bottoms of canyons. The majority of the castellated ruins considered in the following pages are in the proposed Hovenweep National Monument, but there are others in the main Yellow Jacket and its other tributaries.

HOVENWEEP DISTRICT

The name Hovenweep ("Deserted Valley") is an old one in the nomenclature of the canyons of southwestern Colorado and formerly (1877) was applied to the canyon now called the Yellow Jacket, but at present is limited to one of the tributaries. The name is here used to designate an area situated just over the Colorado State line, in Utah, part of which it is hoped will later be reserved from the public domain and made a monument to be called Hovenweep National Monument.

The ruined castles and towers in this district are marvelously well preserved, considering their age and imperfect masonry. We can determine their original appearance with no difficulty and use them in reconstructing the possible forms of more dilapidated ruins, now piles of débris. The best castles and towers known to the author are localized in three canyons: (1) Square Tower Canyon, (2) Holly Canyon, (3) Hackberry Canyon. There are, of course, other castles and towers in the Yellow Jacket-McElmo region, but there is no locality where so many different forms appear in equal numbers in a small area.

RUIN CANYON

The Old Bluff Road from Dolores diverges southward from that to Monticello at Sandstone post office and passes a pile of rocks visible from the road on the Ruin Canyon long before it reaches Square Tower Canyon (fig. 6). This large ruin is situated on the east rim and under it in the side of the cliff are fairly well-preserved cliff-houses. Other ruins with high standing walls were reported in Ruin Canyon but were not visited.

The duplication of names of canyons in this district is misleading. Names like Ruin Canyon are naturally applied to canyons in which there are ruins. When the author learned at Dolores of Ruin Canyon, he supposed it was a tributary of the Yellow Jacket or McElmo, but while the canyon known to cowboys at Dolores by this name has large ruins on its rim, it is not the "Ruin Canyon" to which attention is now directed. The duplication of names has led me to retain the name Ruin Canyon for one and to suggest the name Square Tower Canyon for the other.

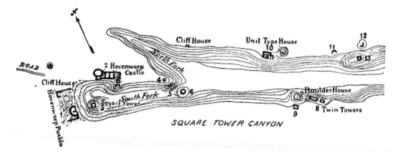

FIG. 6.—Square Tower Canyon.

After leaving Ruin Canyon the Old Bluff Road takes a southerly course, passing through the cedars until a sagebrush clearing replaces the "timber," where it crosses two well-preserved Indian reservoirs, or bare surfaces of rock, dipping south, the southern border having as a retaining wall a low ridge of earth to hold back the water. The retaining wall of the second reservoir has been built up by stockmen and, when the author was there, contained considerable water. Crossing the second reservoir a trail turns east or to the left and follows the road to Keeley Camp, near which are the "Keeley Towers."

At present an automobile can approach within a mile of these ruins.

SQUARE TOWER CANYON

To reach the Square Tower Canyon (pls. 11-17) one returns to the reservoir on the Bluff Road and continues east about 3 miles farther, where a signboard on the left hand indicates the turn off to Square Tower Canyon. Following the new direction about southeast the great buildings are visible a mile away. An automobile can go to the very head of this canyon and a camp can be made within a few feet of Hovenweep House. If the visitor approaches Square Tower Canyon from the McElmo, he passes through Wickyup Canyon, where there are two towers on the summits of elevated buttes, not far from the junction of the canyon and the Yellow Jacket.

The castles and towers in Square Tower Canyon have been known for many years and have been repeatedly photographed.[46]

Several descriptions of these ruins have been printed, but no satisfactory studies of their structure have been published. They are recognized as prehistoric and are generally thought to have been inhabited contemporaneously with the cliff-dwellers of the Mesa Verde, being built in the same style of architecture.

CLASSIFICATION OF RUINS IN SQUARE TOWER CANYON

The ruins in Square Tower Canyon are classified for convenience in description as follows:

(1) Ruins which have indications of inclosed circular kivas, with mural pilasters and banquettes, and closely approximated surrounding rooms. To this class belong ruins 1, 2, and 10. Of these, Unit type Ruin (No. 10) has only one kiva and belongs to the simplest or unit form of the pure type. Ruins 1 and 2 have two or more kivas and are formed by a union of several units, combined with towers and great houses. (2) Ruins, the main feature of which is absence of a circular kiva. The Twin Towers belong to this second or "great house" type. The few cliff-dwellings in this canyon are small, generally without kivas, resembling storage cists rather than domiciles.

HOVENWEEP HOUSE (RUIN 1)

This ruin (fig. 7), the largest in the canyon, is situated at the head of the South Fork. Although many of its walls have fallen, there still remains a semicircular great house (*B*, *C*, *D*) with high walls conspicuous for some distance. The ruin is a pueblo of rectangular form belonging to the pure type, showing circular depressions identified as kivas (*K*), embedded in collections of square and rectangular rooms, and massive walled buildings (*E*) on the south side.

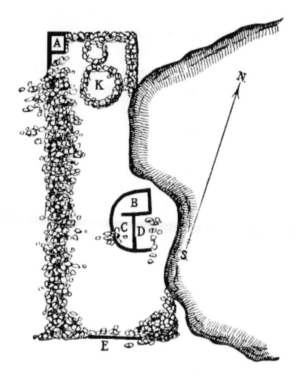

FIG. 7.—Ground plan of Hovenweep House.

The standing walls of the ruin are remains of a conspicuous **D**-shaped tower (**B**, *C*, *D*), which is multichambered. Its straight wall measures 23 feet, the curved wall 56 feet, and its highest wall, which is on the northeast corner, is 15 feet high. At the northwest angle of the ruin (A) there stand remains of high walls which indicate that corner of a rectangular pueblo. Hovenweep House (pl. 14, *a*) was the largest building in this canyon, but with the exception of the addition of a semicircular tower or great house, does not differ greatly from a pueblo like Far View House on the Mesa Verde. The piles of stone and earth indicating rooms below justify the conjecture that when the fallen débris is removed the unfallen walls will still rise several feet above their rocky foundations. If properly excavated, Hovenweep House would be an instructive building, but in its present condition, while very picturesque, its structure is difficult to determine.

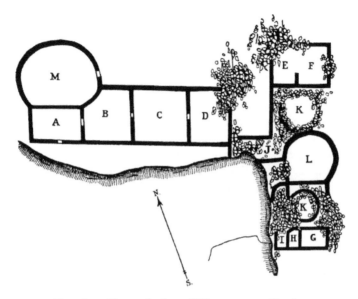

FIG. 8.—Ground plan of Hovenweep Castle.

HOVENWEEP CASTLE

This ruin (pls. 14, b, c; 18, b), like the preceding, has circular kivas compactly embedded in rectangular rooms arranged about them, indicating the pure type of pueblos. The massive walled semicircular towers and great houses are combined with square rooms and kivas, indicating that it is distinguished by two sections, an eastern and a western, which, united, impart to the whole the shape of a letter L (fig. 8).

WESTERN SECTION OF HOVENWEEP CASTLE

The western section (fig. 8, A-D, M) of Hovenweep Castle is made up of five rooms, the most western of which, M, is semicircular, while A, B, C, and D are rectangular. Room A is almost square, one of its walls forming the straight wall of the south side of the semicircular tower, M. At the union its walls are not tied into the masonry of the circular wall of the tower, as may be seen in the illustration, plate 14, b, implying that it was constructed later. There is an entrance into A from the south or cliff side, and a passageway from A to Room B, which latter opens by a doorway into Room C. All rectangular rooms of the western section communicate with each other, but none except A seem to have had an external entrance. The photograph of the south wall of the west section of the ruin (pl. 14, c) shows small portholes in the second story and narrow slits in the tower walls. The lower courses of masonry are formed of thinner stones than the rows above, but smaller stones compose the courses at the top of the wall.

A view of the north wall of the western section (pl. 22, a) shows the tower and rooms united to it. There is no kiva in the western section.

EASTERN SECTION OF HOVENWEEP CASTLE

The longest dimension of the western section (pls. 12, 14, c) is approximately east-west; that of the eastern is nearly north-south. The eastern section (fig. 8, E-L), like the western, has a tower (L), which is situated between two circular depressions or kivas (K). On the north and south ends the eastern section is flanked by rectangular rooms. Those at the north end were better constructed, and even now stand as high as the walls of the western tower. The views show that their corners are not as well preserved as their faces, which is due to defects in masonry, as lack of bonding. Although much débris has accumulated around the kivas, especially in their cavities, it is evident that these ceremonial rooms were formerly one storied, and practically subterranean on account of the surrounding rooms. Several fragments of walls projecting above the accumulated débris indicate rooms at the junction of the eastern and western sections of the ruin, but their form and arrangement at that point are not evident and can be determined only by excavation. The inner kiva walls show evidences of mural pilasters and banquettes like those of cliff-dwellings and other pure pueblo types.

RUIN 3

The square tower (pl. 11, a), standing on a large angular rock in the canyon below Hovenweep Castle, is a remarkable example of prehistoric masonry so situated that it is shut in by cliffs, rendering the outlook limited. Several published photographs of this tower give the impression that it stands in the open and was an outlook, but that this is hardly the case will be seen from a general view looking west up the South Fork.

RUIN 4

This ruin is a small tower situated in a commanding position on the point of the mesa where the canyon forks. The section of the wall still standing indicates a circular form, the north side of which has fallen; the part still intact, or that on the south side, exhibits good masonry about 8 feet high (pl. 15, c).

RUIN 5

The walls of the north segment of a tower stand on a large angular block of stone rising from a ledge above the arroyo, or bed of the canyon, below Ruin 4, on the South Fork. What appears to have been a doorway opens on its north side; this opening is defended by a wall, remains of a former protected passageway into the tower.

On the perpendicular cliff of the precipice near Ruin 5 and below the point on which Ruin 4 stands there are several almost illegible pictographs, below which are rather obscure evidences of a building, the features of which can be determined only by excavation.

Instructive features of Tower No. 5 are two parallel walls, one on each side of the doorway, like those of the circular towers on the promontory at the junction of the Yellow Jacket and McElmo. Other towers on the canyon rim show defensive walls, as in Ruin 9, constructed about their entrances from corners of the buildings to the mesa rim, effectually preventing passage. Morley and Kidder have suggested that the walled recess in the cliff below Ruin 9 was probably built to prevent access from below. This feature is found in the floor entrances of a building near the Great House of the Holly group.

RUIN 6

This ruin is a small tower whose curved walls are so broken down that the form is not evident. It is situated in the base of the talus at the head of the South Fork (pl. 26, a).

ERODED BOWLDER HOUSE
(RUIN 7)

This house, more remarkable from its site than its structure, was constructed in an eroded cave of a bowlder halfway down the talus of the cliff. The front walls are somewhat broken down, but others built in the rear of the cave still remain intact. On the top of the bowlder is the débris of fallen walls, suggesting a former tower, but not much remains in place to determine its outlines. Where the walls are protected the mortar shows impressions of human hands and at one place there are the indentations of a corncob used by the plasterers to press the mortar between the layers of stone. There were formerly at least two rooms in the rear of the cave, the front walls of which have fallen and are strewn down the talus to the bottom of the canyon.

TWIN TOWERS
(RUIN 8)

The so-called Twin Towers, which seen together from certain points appear as one ruin (pl. 15, a, b), rank among the most impressive buildings in Square Tower Canyon. They stand on the south side of the canyon on a rock isolated by a cleft from the adjoining cliff. The larger (fig. 9, A-E) has an oval ground plan and a doorway in the southwest corner; the smaller (F,

G, H, I) is horseshoe shaped with a doorway in the east wall, which is straight. The arrangement of rooms is seen in figure 9. Small walled-up caves are found below the foundation on the northwest base of the larger room.

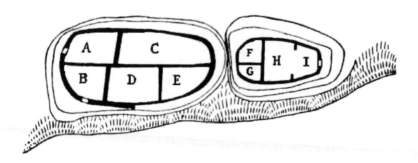

FIG. 9.—Ground plan of Twin Towers.

RUIN 9

The ground plan of this ruin is rectangular in form, 19 feet 6 inches long by 10 feet wide. The standing walls measure 11 feet in altitude. It is situated on the south rim at the mouth of the South Fork, just above Ruin 7, a few feet back from the cliff. A doorway opening in the middle of its north wall was formerly made difficult of entrance by walls, now fallen, extending from the northeast and northwest angles to the edge of the cliff. The masonry throughout is rough; projecting ends of rafters indicate a building two stories high. There are peepholes with plastered surfaces through the southeast and west walls, which suggest ports. A short distance east of the building is a circle of stones reminding the author of a shrine.

UNIT TYPE HOUSE
(RUIN 10)

This pueblo (pl. 19, *c*), from a comparative point of view, is one of the most interesting ruins in the Hovenweep, and is situated on the very edge of the canyon on the North Fork not far from where it begins. It is the simplest form of prehistoric pueblo, or the unit[47] of a pure type, made up of a centrally placed circular ceremonial room (fig. 10, *K*) embedded in rectangular rooms, six in number (*A-F*). The resulting or external form is rectangular, oriented about due north and south; the southern side, which formerly rose from the edge of the canyon, being much broken down and its masonry precipitated over the cliff.

The central kiva (fig. 10) is made of exceptionally fine masonry and shows by what remains that it had mural banquettes, and pilasters to support the roof, with other features like a typical kiva of the Mesa Verde cliff-houses. A side entrance opens in one corner into a small room (fig. 10, G) in which ceremonial objects may have been formerly stored (pl. 32, b).

The kiva of Unit type House is architecturally the same as those with vaulted roofs at Spruce-tree House, Cliff Palace, and Far View House on the Mesa Verde. A similar structure, according to Prudden,[48] occurs at Mitchell Spring Ruin in the Montezuma Valley, and near the Picket corral. The same type was found by Morley[49] at the Cannonball Ruin and by Kidder[50] in a kiva on Montezuma Creek in Utah, where clusters of mounds would appear to be composed of single or composite ruins of this type. This small pueblo was probably inhabited by one social unit, and may be regarded as the first stage of a compound pueblo.

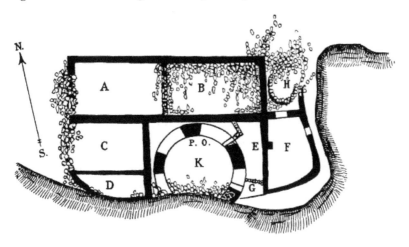

FIG. 10.—Ground plan of Unit type House.

STRONGHOLD HOUSE (RUIN 11)

Ruin 11 is composed of a cluster of several small buildings, one of which is situated on the north edge of the mesa somewhat east of Ruin 10 (pl. 25, b); another, called by Morley and Kidder Gibraltar House, formerly of considerable size, was built on the sloping surface of an angular bowlder (pl. 17, 21, b). Although many walls have fallen, enough remains to render it a picturesque ruin, attractive to the visitor and instructive to the archeologist, by whom it has been classed as a tower. This building from the east appears to be a square tower, but it is in reality composed of several rooms perched on an inaccessible rock.

RUINS IN HOLLY CANYON

The towers in Holly Canyon (fig. 11) are in about the same condition of preservation as those in Square Tower Canyon. They cluster about the head of a small canyon (pl. 18, a) and may be approached on foot along the mesa above Keeley Camp, about a mile distant. Two of the Holly ruins belong to the tower type and were built on fallen bowlders. One of these has two rooms on the ground floor. (Pls. 19, a, b; 20, a, c.)

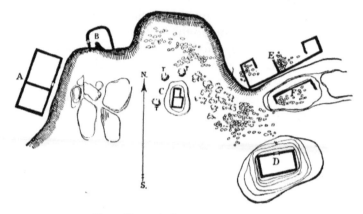

FIG. 11.—Holly Canyon Ruins.

RUIN A, GREAT HOUSE, HACKBERRY CASTLE

Ruin A (pl. 21, a), the largest building of the group, which stands on the edge of the canyon, is rectangular in form, measuring 31 by 9 feet, and is 20 feet high (fig. 11, A). Evidences of two rooms appear on the ground plan, one of which is 14 feet long, the other 12 feet inside measurement. The partition separating the two rooms is not tied into the outer walls, an almost constant feature in ancient masonry. The ends of the rafters are still seen in the wall at a level 12 feet above the base. Fallen stones have accumulated in the rooms to a considerable depth, and the tops of the remaining wall, where the mortar is washed out, will tumble in a short time.

Ruin B (pl. 20, b), situated a short distance north of Ruin A, also stands on the canyon rim. The north wall is entire, but the south wall has fallen. What remains indicates that the ruin was about square, with corners on the north side rounded, imparting to it a semicircular form. The entrance into this room may have been through the floor.

TOWERS [C AND D]

These towers (pl. 23, a, b) show some of the finest masonry known in this region, being constructed on fallen bowlders which their foundations almost completely cover. Holly Tower (pl. 23, b) measures 16 feet high and 21 feet in diameter. It is 7 feet wide, its top rising to a height level with that of the mesa on which stand buildings already considered. One of the two rooms of this tower is narrower and wider than the other, shown in an offset as if constructed at a different time. Its foundations are 17 feet long by 8 feet wide, the highest wall measuring, at the southeast corner, 12 feet 8 inches. There is a fine doorway, wide above and narrow below, in the north wall. The approach at present is difficult on account of the height of the rock on which it stands, but there are evidences of former footholes.

HOLLY HOUSE

Several broken-down walls, some of which are over 6 feet high, situated east of Ruin A, appear to belong to a pueblo of considerable size (fig. 11, E, F), but the large foundation rock on which it is situated has settled, its top having separated from the edge of the canyon, so that the corner of the building (F) is out of plumb. The walls on the adjoining cliff are also much broken down, although several sections of them rise a few feet above the general surface. The cause of this change in level of the base may have been an earthquake or the settling or sliding of the bowlder on the talus down the hill. The united building appears to have been a pueblo of rectangular form. Its walls are so broken down that it was not possible to determine its exact dimensions.

RUINS IN HACKBERRY CANYON

HORSESHOE HOUSE

The large building in Hackberry Canyon, one of the terminal spurs of Bridge Canyon, a mile northeast of the cluster in Holly Canyon, is particularly instructive from the fact that surrounding the remains of a circular tower, for two-thirds of its circumference, is a concentric wall with compartments separated by radial partitions (fig. 12, 1).

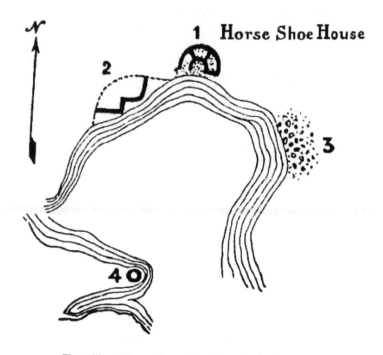

FIG. 12.—Horseshoe (Hackberry) Canyon.

Horseshoe House (pl. 23, c) stands on the north edge of the canyon (fig. 12, 1), having its straight wall on the south side, as is usually the case, the well-preserved north side being curved. The northeastern corner still stands several feet high. The southeastern corner formerly rested on a projecting rock, which recalls the cornerstone of Sun Temple. The masonry of most of the southern segment of the enclosed circular room or tower has fallen down the cliff. There does not appear to have been a doorway on the south side, and there is not space for rooms on this side on account of the nearness to the edge of the cliff. While the form (fig. 13) of Horseshoe Ruin recalls that of Sun Temple, in details of room structure it is widely divergent. The length of the south wall, or that connecting the two ends of the horseshoe, is 30 feet, its width 27 feet; the highest wall on the northwest side is 12 feet. Figure 13 shows the arrangement of the rooms and the mutilation of the south wall of the ruin. The distance between the outer and inner concentric walls averages 4 feet; the circular room is 17 feet in diameter.

In the same cluster as Horseshoe Ruin (pl. 24, a) there is another well-made tower (fig. 12, 4), constructed on a point at the entrance to the canyon, and below it in a cave are well-preserved walls of a cliff-dwelling.

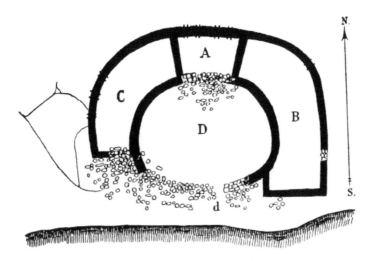

FIG. 13.—Ground plan of Horseshoe House.

A short distance due north of Horseshoe House, at the head of a small canyon, a tributary of Bridge Canyon, there are two large pueblos and a round tower. The pueblos are mentioned by Prudden, who gives a ground plan which indicates an extensive settlement.

TOWERS IN THE MAIN YELLOW JACKET CANYON

Of the several towers and great houses of the main Yellow Jacket Canyon two may suffice to show their resemblance to those in Square Tower Canyon. The two towers considered belong to the **D**-shaped variety, the straight wall, as is almost always the case, being on the south side.

DAVIS TOWER

Mr. C. K. Davis, who lives not far from the Yellow Jacket Spring, conducted the author to a tower of semicircular ground plan (fig. 14) near his ranch. This ruin (pl. 26, *b*), is situated on a rocky ridge on top of the talus halfway down to the bottom of the canyon, on its right side.

LION (LITTRELL) TOWER[51]

This tower (pl. 29, *b*) is built on a bowlder situated in Yellow Jacket Canyon a mile from Mr. Littrell's ranch and about 5 miles south of the Yellow Jacket post office; approximately 20 miles from Dolores, Colorado. Its ground plan (fig. 15) is **D**-shaped, the lower story being divided by partitions into four rooms. The wall of the middle room seems to be double, or to have been reenforced. It measures 40 feet on the straight side, the highest wall being about 25 feet above the base. The foundations rest on the irregular surface of a bowlder to which it conforms.

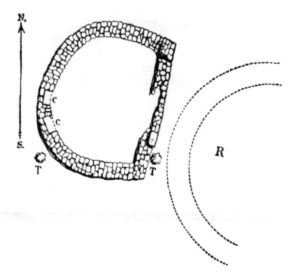

FIG. 14.—Ground plan of Davis Ruin.

M'LEAN BASIN

McLean Basin is 3 miles from the Old Bluff City Road near Picket corral, 32 miles from Dolores. It has been a favorite wintering place for stock and is well known to herdsmen. One can approach the ruin from the road to Bluff City and the towers here referred to are easily reached by a trail down the mesa to the highest terrace. There are said to be several ruins in the McLean Basin, the two towers (pls. 26, c, 27, 28, a, b) visited being placed in an exceptional position in reference to surrounding rooms. One of these towers is circular, the other **D**-shaped or semicircular in ground plan (fig. 16, A, B).

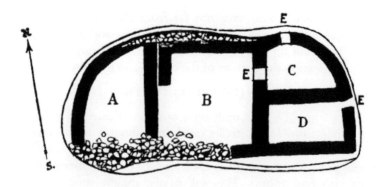

FIG. 15.-Ground plan of Lion House.

Previously to the author's study of the southwestern towers two forms of these structures were recognized; the square or rectangular, and the circular or oval. It is now known that several of the towers previously described as circular are in reality **D**-shaped, and this form is probably more common than the circular.

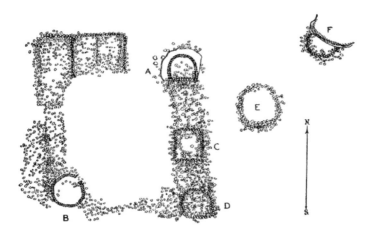

FIG. 16.—Ground plan of ruin with towers in McLean Basin.

The rectangular building in the McLean Basin has a circular tower (pl. 28, b) on the southwest angle and a **D**-shaped tower (pl. 28, a) on the northeast. They resemble two turrets rising above the remaining walls that form the sides of the rectangles. These towers average about 12 feet high, and are well constructed, while low connecting walls of coarse masonry rise slightly above the surface. It would appear from the amount of débris that the remaining walls indicate a row of buildings, one story high, with circular subterranean kivas, but this can not be accurately determined without excavation of the ruin. Outside of the rectangle, however, there are at least two circular areas, possibly kiva pits. The rectangular building measures about 50 feet square. The ground on which the buildings formerly stood slopes to the south, and back of it on the north rises a low perpendicular bluff which effectually shelters it in that direction. The union of a circular and a semicircular tower with, a rectangular ruin is a feature not common in the McElmo-Yellow Jacket region but appears in Hovenweep Castle, elsewhere described. Lower down the sides of the basin and near by are many indications of walls of buildings.

The pottery in the neighborhood belongs to the same black and white types commonly found in the Hovenweep and Mesa Verde areas.

Except for their peculiar relation to the rectangular building the McLean towers do not differ essentially from others, which leads to the inference that they were used contemporaneously and for the same purpose. There is a well-made doorway (fig. 17) in the Round Tower.

TOWER IN SAND CANYON

Sand Canyon, which opens into McElmo Canyon near Battle Rock, has several types of prehistoric ruins, viz, towers, cliff-houses, and large rim-rock pueblos. The tower type of architecture represented by the example here figured (pl. 5, a) is isolated from other forms of buildings. This tower is figured by Doctor Prudden, who mentions another in the neighborhood which the author did not visit.

TOWERS IN ROAD (WICKYUP) CANYON

FIG. 17.—Doorway in Round Tower, McLean Basin.

The nomenclature of the northern canyons of the McElmo has considerably changed in the last 40 years. What we now call the Yellow Jacket was formerly known through its entire course as the Hovenweep. A small canyon opening near its mouth, now known as Road Canyon, was formerly called the Wickyup. The Old Bluff City Road from Dolores, Colorado, to Bluff City, Utah, divides into two branches a short distance before it descends into the McElmo, its left branch passing through Road Canyon, the right bank of which follows the Yellow Jacket, which the traveler fords a short distance above its junction with the McElmo.

Wickyup Canyon may be called picturesque, its cliffs being worn into fantastic shapes by water and sand. It has important antiquities, among the most striking of which are two towers (pl. 24, b), crowning the tops of low buttes or hills. The walls of these towers are well constructed, one being a simple structure with a single room, the other having appended rectangular rooms extending toward the northwest, some distance along a ridge of rocks. An examination of these two towers, which are about one-quarter of a mile apart, shows that they belong to the same type as the simple forms of those above mentioned, and as the entrance to Square Tower Canyon is not far away, they probably belong to the same series. The first of the towers, called "Bowlder Castle," is situated a few hundred feet east of the road, from which it is easily seen. This ruin is rectangular in shape and rises from a basal mass of débris indicating broken-down walls of rooms. At a level with the top of this débris on its southern side stands a well-constructed tower with well-made doorway, the threshold and lintel of which are smooth stones, whose edges project slightly from the surface of the wall. One remarkable feature of this tower is that the doorway has been walled up with rude secondary masonry (pl. 25, a). The south wall of this building has tumbled over, as is usually the case, but the north wall rises several feet above the base. The masonry of the second tower is also broken down on the south side, but the standing remains of the north wall, which is circular, are over 10 feet high. The indications are that the ground plan of this building was oval in shape and that it inclined inward slightly from foundation to apex. Scattered over the surface are the remnants of fallen walls, and near it there is a well-marked depression, not unlike those found in unit type mounds, indicating kivas.

TOWERS OF THE MANCOS

The author's examination of the towers in the region considered embraced likewise a few in the Mancos Canyon and valley. In all essential features the Mancos towers resemble those of Mesa Verde, the McElmo, and the Yellow Jacket Canyons, and were evidently built by the same people who constructed the towers on Navaho Canyon and elsewhere on the Mesa Verde National Park. A brief reference to two or three of these Mancos River towers may suffice to point out their general structure.

HOLMES TOWER

One of the towers figured by Holmes in 1877 is still among the best preserved in this region and can be visited by following up the Mancos Canyon from the west about 10 miles from where the Cortez road crosses the Mancos River before going on to Ship-rock. There is at this point a bridge and near the crossing an industrial farm of the Ute Reservation where accommodations were obtained. The Mancos Valley widens after leaving the canyon, the southern side of Mesa Verde appearing as a series of high mesas separated by canyons. In the neighborhood of the western end of Mesa Verde are lofty buttes, one called Chimney Rock, another the Ute Woman. This valley and the canyons extending into the Mesa Verde contain numerous piles of stone indicative of buildings of rectangular shape with numerous circular depressions. No cluster of mounds like those in Montezuma Valley was seen, but about 40 sites of buildings were distributed at intervals. None of these have standing walls above ground.

Following up the Mancos Canyon is a wagon about 9 miles an arroyo was encountered and from there horses were taken and the river crossed to its south bank, above which, on the shelving terrace, is the Holmes Tower, visible many miles down the canyon. This tower (pl. 29, *a*) is in much the same condition as when sketched by Holmes over 40 years ago. It is circular in form, about 10 feet in diameter, and about 16 feet high, with a broken window on the north side. The sky line is irregular. It is one of the best preserved towers, but not as high or as well constructed as some of the Hovenweep specimens.

Accompanying this tower on the north there are mounds indicative of rooms and two circular saucer-like depressions. Excavations revealing a few human bones, including a well-worn human skull, have been made in a burial place southeast of the tower, where the surface is covered with fragments of pottery. Except in size Holmes Tower does not differ from others already described, but, like them, is connected with rectangular rooms. Farther up the Mancos Canyon there are other towers, one of which, Great Tower, is mentioned by Holmes in his report.

On the way up the canyon, perhaps two-thirds of the distance from the bridge to the Holmes Tower, midway in the alluvial plain and on the right bank of Mancos Creek, stands a circular ruin which conforms to Holmes's description of Great Tower but is too poorly preserved to be positively identified. All that now remains of this building is a large pile of rocks with a central depression, but no signs of radiating partitions, although such may have existed when it was constructed and for many years after it began to fall into ruin.

TOWERS ON THE MANCOS RIVER
BELOW THE BRIDGE

TOWER A

There are two towers situated on the south side of the Mancos below the bridge on the Ship-rock Road, one about 6, the other 7 miles distant. The walls of the first of these (pl. 30, *b*) are visible for some distance and are about 6 feet high, evidently very much broken down on the south and east sides. Its shape is round and there is a pile of stones indicating rooms on the east side separated from the tower by a depression. It would be a valuable contribution to our knowledge of these ruins if some one would determine the nature of these pits, which can hardly be regarded as reservoirs, but suggest kivas.

TOWER B

The tower (pl. 31, *a*) situated farther down the Mancos River has a more commanding position than Tower A and is conspicuous because it stands on a projecting precipice, below the rim of which are walled-up artificial caves. These caves have apparently never been entered by white men; the walls of masonry are unbroken and there are square openings, windows or doorways, which can be made out long before reaching the place.

This tower (pl. 30, *a*) is almost perfectly round, about 10 feet in diameter, and stands at least 6 feet high. The south wall has fallen. In the pile of rocks on that side may be readily seen the top of a straight wall reaching to the edge of the cliff as if for protection, but no other fallen walls may now be seen in the neighborhood. The face of the cliff below this tower (pls. 7, *b*; 31, *b*) is almost perpendicular, the component strata of soft shale alternating with harder rocks, the former well fitted for artificial excavations.

The author was not impressed with the idea that any considerable number of troglodytic inhabitants dwelt in the small cliff rooms (pl. 31, *b*)[52] dug in it. Farther on there are other caves the walls of the entrance to which are still in sight. It is true the surface of the cliff may have been eroded and fallen in the time since they were abandoned. They appeared to be storage cists rather than inhabited rooms.

Along the valley by the side of the road down the Mancos from the bridge to the ruins many heaps of stone were noticed in the valley but none of these were extensive or had walls standing above ground. Nor were they arranged in clusters as is common in the Montezuma Valley. On top of these heaps were found large fragments of slag in which was embedded charred corn, indicating a great fire. Similar slag also with burnt corn has often been found by the author on the floor of excavated rooms.

MEGALITHIC AND SLAB HOUSE RUINS AT MCELMO BLUFF

The ruined walls on the bluff situated at the junction of the McElmo and Yellow Jacket Canyons are archeologically instructive. As the mesa between the two canyons narrows in a promontory, about 100 feet in altitude, its configuration reminds one of the East Mesa of the Hopi. It is inaccessible on three sides, but on the fourth, where the width of the mesa is contracted, there are remains of a low zigzag wall, extending from one side to the other. At the western base of this promontory, on the ledge higher than the river, there are artificial walls built on bowlders in the sides of which shallow caves are eroded and near by them circular depressions. There are likewise remains of a small pueblo with walls much broken down and across the river the ruins of a community house, one of the largest in the district. The exceptional character of the ruins on top of this promontory has been mentioned or described by several visitors, as Holmes, Jackson, and Morley and Kidder, and various conjectures have been made as to their character and relation to the other ruins in this neighborhood.

The ruins on this mesa are of two kinds: small inclosures made of slabs of stone set on edge and semicircular structures (fig. 18), also constructed of upright stone slabs or megaliths. Three of the latter have concentric surrounding walls with a "vestibule" entrance (?) at the south somewhat like rooms at the bases of towers. One of these is said by Morley and Kidder to have three concentric walls. The small box-like structures are numerous, and are rudely constructed, united in an imperfect ring about the circular rooms.

In verification of the various theories that have been suggested to account for these rectangular structures—their interpretation as storage bins, burial places, and cremation rooms—we have no proof. Similar rooms of megaliths exist on Sandstone Canyon and at other places to the north and in Montezuma Canyon to the west. The rude, massive character of the masonry leads me to refer them to the slab house culture of Kidder and the imperfect masonry suggests they were habitations in a period antedating that of the pure pueblo culture. Such fragments of pottery as were found were, like the architecture, rude and archaic, adding weight to the interpretation that they belonged to a very old epoch.

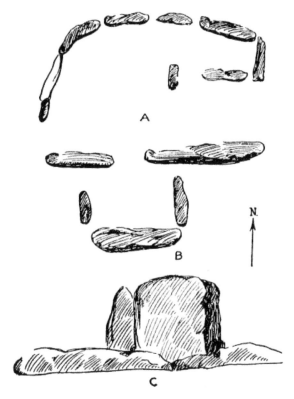

FIG. 18.—Megalithic stone inclosure, McElmo Bluff.

The author regards the structures made of stones set on edge as very old, possibly examples of the most primitive buildings in the McElmo region, antedating the pueblos with horizontal masonry farther east. West of the mouth of the Yellow Jacket, especially on the Montezuma Mesa, these megalithic walls are more pretentious, as if this was the center of the earlier phase of house buildings. In the eastern ruins these slabs of stone set on edge sometimes appear as at Far View House with horizontal masonry, but more as a survival.

Since their discovery and description by Jackson and Holmes 40 years ago, little has been added to our knowledge of these inclosures, although similar remains have been reported at various points from Dolores far into Utah. They are called cemeteries and crematories by the farmers and stockmen, but skeletons or burnt bones do not occur in them; the charcoal shows wood fiber, and is not bone ash. More knowledge must be obtained through excavations before their significance can be determined. Their association with circular rooms appears in Jackson's account[53] of the stone structures on the promontory at the mouth of the Yellow Jacket. He says:

"The perpendicular scarp of the mesa ran round very regularly, 50 to 100 feet in height, the talus sloping down at a steep angle. On cave-like benches at the foot of the scarp is a row of rock shelters, much ruined, in one of which was found a very perfect polished-stone implement. Gaining the top of the mesa with some difficulty, we found a perfectly flat surface, 100 yards in width by about 200 in length, separated from the main plateau by a narrow neck, across which a wall had been thrown, but which is now nearly leveled. Almost the entire space fenced in by this wall was covered by an extended series of small squares, formed by thin slabs of sand-rock set on end. All were uniform in size, measuring about 3 by 5 feet, and arranged in rows, two and three deep, adjusted to various points of the compass. There were also a few circles disposed irregularly about the inclosed area, each about 20 feet in diameter, their circumferences being formed of similar rectangular spaces, leaving a circular space of 10 feet diameter in the center. These rectangles occur mainly in groups, and are found indiscriminately scattered through the whole region that has come under our observation upon the mesa tops and in the valleys. They all have the same general shape and size, and are seldom accompanied by even the faintest indication of a mound-like character. We have always supposed them to be graves, but have not as yet found any evidence that would prove them such. Some that we excavated to the depth of 5 and 6 feet in a solid earth that had never been disturbed did not reward our search with the faintest vestige of human remains. In nearly every case, however, a thin scattered layer of bits of charcoal was found from 6 to 18 inches beneath the surface. In one instance, near the Mesa Verde, the upright slabs of rock which inclosed one of these rectangles were sunk 2 feet into the earth and projected 6 inches above it."

Holmes (op. cit., pp. 385-386) describes similar structures:

"The greater portion of what are supposed to be burial places occur on the summits of hills or on high, barren promontories that overlook the valleys and cañons. In these places considerable areas, amounting in some cases to half an acre or more, are thickly set with rows of stone slabs, which are set in the ground and arranged in circles or parallelograms of greatly varying dimensions. At first sight the idea of a cemetery is suggested, although on examination it is found that the soil upon the solid rock surfaces is but a few inches deep, or if deeper, so compact that with the best implements it is very difficult to penetrate it.

"On the west bank of the Dolores, near the second bend, I came upon a cluster of these standing stones on the summit of a low, rounded hill, and in the midst of a dense growth of full-grown piñon pines."

The rows of stones at this place, according to the same author, were composed of undressed slabs, many of which had fallen, the parallelograms averaging 3 by 8 feet in dimensions. Thin layers of bits of charcoal and pottery occur in the neighborhood. The date these slabs were placed upright was very early, for trees growing in the inclosures were estimated to be three or four hundred years old. These stones were sometimes "embedded in the sides and roots of the trees." Holmes had the "impression that these places, if not actually burying grounds, were at least places used for the performance of funeral rites ... the remains of the dead being burned or left to decay in the open air."

The interiors of the inclosures were found on excavation to be filled to a depth of about a foot with soil mixed with ashes. There were many fragments of pottery, and some other objects near them, but nothing to indicate, as suggested by previous observations, that they were burial cists or even crematories for burying the dead. No charred human remains occur, but charcoal is abundant. It may have been that these places were used as ovens for roasting corn or for some culinary purposes, the neighboring circular rooms being possibly used for the same purposes as towers by the people who formerly inhabited this region. They are not large enough for dwellings and the soil in them is too shallow for burial purposes. They belong to a type which is widely distributed over the district visited by the author. Especially fine examples occur north of Sandstone Canyon district.

At the base of the great cliff, on the top of which the remains in question are found, under the shelter of an overhanging bowlder, may be seen one of the finest collections of pictographs of animals and human beings. Not far from the last-mentioned bowlder the walls of a large pueblo can readily be traced along the banks of the McElmo Canyon. In his studies of the antiquities of this region the author did not penetrate west of the mouth of Yellow Jacket Canyon, but he was told by stockmen and sheep herders of the existence of many other ruins contiguous to the road all the way from this point to Bluff City. The most important of these have already been described in a general way.

GRASS MESA CEMETERY

Grass Mesa, a plateau with precipitous sides overlooking the Dolores River, is about 10 miles down the river from Dolores on the right bank of the stream. There remain few signs of former buildings at this place, but very many artifacts, pottery, stone implements, and fragments of well-worn metates occur at various places, some of which are among the best ever seen by the author. This bluff seems to have been the site of a settlement, possibly pre-Puebloan, like that on McElmo Bluff, with rough walls, resorted to for refuge, and later used as a cemetery. It is well adapted for these purposes, its top being almost inaccessible on the river side. There are many other similar sites of Indian settlements farther down the river, but this is one of the most typical. The scenery along the road that follows the banks of the river from Dolores is ever to be remembered on account of high cliffs on each side.

RESERVOIRS

Many artificial reservoirs dating to prehistoric times were observed in the area covered by the author's reconnoissance. These fall into two well-marked types, one form being a circular depression, apparently excavated and sometimes walled up with earth or stones. The other form was not excavated by man, but the sloping surface of rock was surrounded on the lowest level by a bank of earth, forming a dam or retaining wall. Both types of reservoirs are commonly formed near some former center of population, but sometimes occur far from mounds, wherever the surface of the land has a convenient slope and the water can be compounded by a retaining wall. The height of the bank that holds back the water of these prehistoric reservoirs has been increased in some cases by stockmen; the walls of others still remain practically the same height they were when constructed by the aborigines. One of the best examples of the second type of reservoir, the retaining wall of which is shown in plate 32, a, is crossed by the road to Bluff City near the ruins in Holly Canyon, not far from Picket corral. A few miles north of this reservoir, at the edge of the cedars, the road crosses another of these ancient reservoirs, whose retaining bank has been considerably increased in height by stockmen. The ancient reservoir at Bug Mesa covers fully 4 acres, and the reservoir near Goodman Point Ruin is almost as large, and, although somewhat changed from its aboriginal condition, is still used by farmers dwelling in the neighborhood. The latter belongs to the first type; the former to the second. Reservoirs of one or the other type are generally found in the neighborhood of all large heaps of rocks, the so-called mounds that indicate the former existence of pueblos. The reservoir of the Mummy Lake village on the Mesa Verde belongs to the excavated type.

PICTOGRAPHS

At many places covered by this reconnoissance there were found interesting collections of engraved figures of ancient date cut on bowlders or vertical cliffs. These are generally situated in the neighborhood of ruins, but sometimes exist far from human remains. They generally have geometrical forms, rectangular and spiral predominating. Associated with these occur also representations of human beings, birds, and animals, and figures of bird tracks, human hands, and bear claws. There is a remarkable similarity in all these figures which sometimes occur on the stones composing the masonry of the buildings which indicates they were contemporaneous. They were pecked on the stones with rude stone chisels, but as a rule show no indication of paint. None of these figures could be regarded, without the wildest flights of the imagination, as letters or hieroglyphics, and there is no indication that inscriptions were intended. Their general character, as shown in a cluster (pl. 33), indicates rather clan symbols; in some instances spiral forms were probably made to indicate the presence of water. The incised figures on the walls of buildings were probably decorative in character, the first efforts of primitive man to embellish the walls of his dwellings, an art which reached a very high development in Mexico and Central America. There are, however, indications that these figures were covered with plaster and were therefore invisible, so that we might suppose them to be masons' signs, indicating the clan kinship of those who constructed the walls. Perhaps the largest group of these pictographs occurs on an eroded bowlder near the mouth of the Yellow Jacket Canyon, just below the great promontory separating it from the McElmo, on the surface of which are the remarkable dwellings composed of slabs of stone set on edge. Another large cluster, the members of which are of the same general style as that already mentioned, was seen in Sandstone Canyon, a few miles south of the road from Dolores to Monticello. There are several groups of pictographs in the neighborhood of the large towers elsewhere described. The most noteworthy of these is situated at the head of the south fork of Square Tower Canyon on a vertical cliff below the ruined Tower No. 4. The face of the cliff is very much eroded, and the figures are in places almost illegible. They consist of bird designs, accompanied with figures of snakes, rain clouds, and other designs, portions of which are obliterated and impossible of determination. As a rule, these pictographs resemble very closely those in the cliff-houses of the Mesa Verde and add their evidence of a uniformity of art design in these two regions.

In addition to pictographs cut on the surface of the cliff, we also find in sheltered caves others not incised but with indications of color, showing the former existence of painted figures. Some of these, however, are not ascribed to the Indians who built the towers, but to a later tribe who camped in this region after the house builders had disappeared. They were probably made by wandering bands of Ute Indians, and are not significant in a comparison of the different kinds of buildings described in this article.

MINOR ANTIQUITIES

The preceding pages deal wholly with the immovable antiquities, as buildings, reservoirs, and the like. In addition to these evidences of a former population, there should be mentioned likewise the smaller antiquities, as pottery, stone objects, weapons, baskets, fabrics, bone and other implements. No excavation was attempted in the course of the reconnoissance, so that this chapter in the author's report is naturally a very brief one. The few statements which follow are mainly based on local collections, one of which, owned by Mr. Williamson, of the First National Bank of Dolores, is comprehensive. The most suggestive of these minor antiquities are objects of burnt clay or pottery, which occur generally in piles of débris or accompany human burials. It was the custom of these people, like the cliff-dwellers, to deposit, near the dead, food in bowls and other household utensils, varying in shape, technique, decoration, and color. The most important fact regarding these ceramics is that they belong to the same archaic type as those from the ruins of the Mesa Verde. The predominating colors are white or gray with black figures, within and without, almost universally geometrical in form. There occurs also a relatively large number of corrugated vessels, and those made by using coils of clay, the figures on their exterior being indented with some implement, as a bone, stone, or even with the finger nail. While the majority belong to the black-and-white group, the red ware decorated with black figures is found but comparatively rarely, which is also true of the pottery of the cliff-dwellers. In the large variety of forms of burnt clay objects, the most remarkable in shape is a double water jar, connected by a transverse tube, the ends of which project beyond the opening into the jar, much in the form of an animal with a head at one end, body elongated, terminating in a short tail, the legs not being represented. While the number of unbroken mortuary bowls obtained from this region thus far known is comparatively small, we find in many places large quantities of broken fragments, all of which belong to the varieties of ware above enumerated.

None of the bowls, vases, dippers, or other ceramic objects from the region of the ruins described have that significant feature commonly called the "life line;" the encircling lines are continuous around the vessel, and not broken at one point. The broken line never occurs on archaic pottery like black-and-white ware, and we may accept the hypothesis that the conception which gave rise to it was foreign to the people of the Mesa Verde and adjacent areas. It would be instructive to map out the distribution of this custom which was so prevalent in pottery from the Gila and Little Colorado and its tributaries, and absent in that from ruins on the San Juan and Mimbres. It occurs in ware from certain Rio Grande prehistoric ruins, as if it were a connecting link with the ancient culture of the Little Colorado.

Of the stone implements found in this region the most characteristic is the celt called *tcamahia* which is not found in regions not affected by the San Juan culture. These objects are found from Mesa Verde to the Hopi pueblos.[54] A peculiar form of prehistoric chipped chert implement occurs at Mesa Verde and elsewhere in the area. A flint knife in the Williamson collection at Dolores was purchased from a Ute woman who said it was found on a ruin. She wore it attached to her belt by a buckskin thong fastened to a bead-worked cover.

Bone objects were mainly needles, dirks, and bodkins, presenting in the main no essential differences from those repeatedly described, especially by Nordenskiöld in his important memoir on the cliff-dwellers of the Mesa Verde. Objects made of marine shell are rare. The presence of flattened slabs of stone or metates showing on the surface evidences of grinding occur with human bones in many localities, indicating either that a custom still extant among the Pueblos of burying the metates with the dead was observed, or that the burials were made under floors of these long-abandoned houses. It would seem, on the former hypothesis, that these objects were buried with the women, but as the condition of the skeletal remains is poor the sex could not be determined by direct observation.

The unprotected nature of the sites and the condition of the ruins prevented the preservation of fragile articles like baskets and fabrics, which frequently occur in caves, in one or two instances buried under the floors. There is little doubt that excavations in cemeteries of the open-sky ruins would reveal considerable material of this nature, which would probably duplicate that which has been produced from the adjacent cliff-houses. Many parts of wooden beams, mainly the remains of flooring and roofs, were seen still in the walls, but these as a rule were fragmentary. The ends of the timbers still adhering to the walls show that they were cut into shape by stone implements, aided by live embers. They appear to have been split by means of wedges made of stone and often rubbed down smooth with polishing instruments of the same material. The majority of these wooden beams plainly show the action of fire, but no roof was intact. From the size of the logs shown in fragments of beams, it is evident that the roof supports had been brought there from some distance; trees of the magnitude they imply do not now grow in the neighborhood of some of the ruins where these beams occur.

HISTORIC REMAINS

The various objects found in the ruins or on the surface of the ground as a rule are characteristic of a people in the stone-age culture, ignorant of metals, and therefore prehistoric, but here and there on the surface have been picked up iron weapons which belonged to the historic period. The old "Spanish Trail" mentioned in preceding pages was the early highway from Santa Fe, New Mexico, to the Great Salt Lake, and followed approximately an old Indian trail that was probably used by the prehistoric inhabitants or the builders of the towers. Not far from the head of Yellow Jacket Canyon a ranchman discovered on his farm a few years ago the blades of two Spanish iron lance heads or knives, still well preserved, the hilts, however, being destroyed. These objects, now in Mr. Williamson's collection at Dolores, may have belonged to a party of Spanish soldiers who explored this region, but their form, in addition to the material, is so characteristic that no one would assign them to aboriginal manufacture. Fragments of a stirrup of metal, parts of the harness or saddle, also belonging to the Spanish epoch, have also been found. The indications are that these objects are historic, but their owners may have been Indians who obtained them from Europeans. They probably do not antedate the middle of the eighteenth century, when two Catholic fathers, with an escort of soldiers, made their trip of discovery from Santa Fe into what is now Utah. They shed no light on the epoch of the aborigines who constructed the castles and towers considered in this paper.

CONCLUSIONS

In the preceding pages the author has considered several different types of buildings, which, notwithstanding their variety in forms, have much in common and can be interpreted as indicating an identical phase of pueblo development. A comparative study of their distribution shows us that they occur in a well-defined geographical area. In comparison with stone buildings in other parts of the Southwestern States, this phase shows superior masonry. It is considered as chronologically antedating the historic epoch and post-dating an earlier, and as yet not clearly defined, phase out of which it sprung in the natural evolution from simple to complex forms.

These buildings express the communal thought of the builders, since they were constructed by groups of people rather than by individuals. Architecture representing the thoughts of many minds is conservative, or less liable to innovation or departure from prescribed forms and methods. These community houses express the thought of men in groups at different times, and, so far as archeology teaches, are the best exponents of what we call contemporary social conditions, while pottery and other small portable objects, being products of individual endeavor, furnish little on social organization, or general cultural conditions of communities. Although determination of cultural areas built on identity of pottery often coincides with those determined by buildings, this is not always the case. Specialized culture areas determined by highly conventionalized designs on ceramics are localized, more numerous, and as a rule more modern. Hence a culture area determined by architectural features may include several subareas determined by pottery.

The author has thought it possible to differentiate two distinct epochs or phases of house building in the upper part of the San Juan drainage, viz. the early and the middle stages of development. There are included in the early condition certain crude architectural efforts similar to the non-Pueblos represented in regions adjoining the Pueblo area. This early condition, though not clearly defined, is beginning to be revealed by intensive studies of the so-called slab house dwellings and isolated brush houses. Evidences of this stage have been found in several localities, as on McElmo Bluff, or combined with walls of what may be called true pueblo buildings. The differences between some of the buildings of the early stage and those of the aborigines in southern California, or of the Utes and Shoshonean tribes, are slight; resemblances which point to relations are not considered in detail.

From their advance in house building, it has been commonly stated that the Pueblo people were either derived from Mexican tribes or, as was customary in the seventeenth and eighteenth centuries to suppose, their descendants had made their way south and developed into the more advanced Mexican culture as the Aztecs. These conclusions are not supported by comparison with available architectural data observed among these two peoples. The basal error is the mistake in considering the earth houses of the Gila the same as pueblos. The habitations of the Gila compounds were structurally different from pueblos, and their sanctuaries or ceremonial rooms had not the same form or relation to the dwellings. The Gila compounds are allied to Mexican buildings; but there is little in common between them and pure pueblos. The same is true of the type of stone dwellings on the Verde, Tonto, and Little Colorado. Certain likenesses exist between the Casas Grandes of the Gila and those of Mexico, although little relationship exists between the temples or ceremonial buildings of the valley of Mexico and the Casas Grandes of the Gila. The architecture of the Pueblos and the Aztecs is very different; the habitations of Mexican tribes resemble those of the Gila. The forms[55] of ceremonial chambers differ, one being rectangular mounds or pyramids, the other circular, generally subterranean.

Rather than seek the origin of the house builders of the San Juan, or the parent Pueblos, from Mexican sources, the author believes the custom of building stone houses in the pueblo region was not derived from any locality not now included in the pueblo area, but it developed as an autochthonous growth, the earliest stages as well as the most complex forms being of local origin. Incoming Indians may have introduced ideas of foreign birth but they did not bring in the mason's craft. That custom developed in the Southwest, where we find the whole series from a single stone-house or a cave with walls closing the entrance to the most highly developed architectural production north of Mexico. There are cliff-dwellings in many other localities in the world but there are nowhere, except in the region here considered, cliff-dwellings with circular kivas constructed on this unique plan. It is generally supposed that a type of room called "small house" was the predecessor of the multiple community dwelling throughout the Southwest. This type, defined as a simple four-walled, one story building with a flat roof, is widely spread in New Mexico and Arizona. The strongest arguments in favor of its greater antiquity are possibly its simplicity of form and the character of accompanying ceramics—corrugated, black-and-white, and red pottery. Characteristic small houses of the Mesa Verde and McElmo Canyon belong to the same type of pueblo as the largest extensive villages which are more complicated than the so-called small house. It is what the author has called the pure type which is structurally different from the "small house," the so-called archaic form of the mixed pueblos of the Rio Grande. This unit type is likewise unlike the small house of the Little Colorado, including those of the Zuñi Valley and the Hopi Wash, although the Hopi kivas show the influence of the Mesa Verde culture in the persistence of the ceremonial opening in the floor called the sipapu.

A cluster of small houses or the village such as we find at Mummy Lake on the Mesa Verde is composed of several scattered members, each containing for the religious and secular life the "pure type" rooms constructed on the same plan. In a village like the Aztec Spring House several unit buildings are united, forming one community house larger than the rest, which was the dominant one of the village, the remaining houses being smaller and scattered. Aztec Spring, Mitchell Spring, and Mud Spring villages show a similar consolidation of units with outlying smaller houses, and the number of units in such a union is believed to be indicated by the number of circular rooms, or kivas. Thus, four kivas might be supposed to indicate four consolidated social units.

The complete concentration of several unit pueblos into one or more large communal buildings[56] is also found in several cases in the area we have studied, but we must look to the great ruin at Aztec or those on the Chaco Canyon for examples of almost complete amalgamation. Thus these large pueblos where an almost complete consolidation has occurred have resulted from a fusion or condensation of what might have formerly been a rambling village composed of several separate units. This clustering of small separated houses in a village is not peculiar to the San Juan but exists elsewhere in the Southwest, as in the Rio Grande region, where, however, the structure of each component small house is different. These separate mounds do not indicate the unit type as defined, and the Rio Grande pueblo of modern date has its kiva separated from the house masses, which have grouped themselves in rectangular lines or rooms surrounding courts. There are, perhaps, examples in this region where a circular kiva is found embedded in house masses, but these are so few in number that they may possibly be regarded as incorporate survivals due to acculturation.

In the Gila Valley compounds, as Casa Grande, and on the Little Colorado, the unit type is unknown. Several blocks of buildings on the Gila are surrounded by a rectangular wall which is wanting in ruins of the Little Colorado and its tributaries. Here one of the units may be enlarged, following in some respects the conditions at Aztec Spring Ruin. A surrounding wall also appears in some of the Pueblo villages and pueblos, but when we compare one of the units of a Casa Grande compound with that of a Montezuma Valley village, we find little in common, the main difference, so far as form is concerned, being the absence of a circular kiva.[57] There is nothing in a Gila Valley compound we can structurally call a circular kiva, and no morphological equivalent of the circular kiva in ruins on the tributaries of the Salt and Gila. On the horizon of the Gila culture area there are no circular kivas, due to acculturation. There are rooms analogous to kivas used for ceremonials at Hopi and Zuñi, but they are not true kivas as we have interpreted them in the San Juan area. Both Hopi and Zuñi are composite people and have elements derived from Gila and Pueblo influences, but neither belong to the pure type in the sense the author defines it.

The author has attempted to show that the structure of the houses whose clustering composes villages in the Montezuma Valley is the same as that of Far View House of the Mummy Lake village on top of Mesa Verde; and that these architectural resemblances are close enough to indicate that the villages of the two localities were inhabited by people of the same general culture. He has proved that the pure type of such a village as shown in Far View House was constructed on the same plan as a cliff-dwelling, notwithstanding one is built in the open, the other in a cave. The geographic extension of this type has been traced into Utah. Ruined pueblos on the Chaco Canyon or at Aztec on the Animas, which is geographically nearer the Mesa Verde, are more concentrated but indicate the same culture. Renewed research is necessary to determine the southern and western extension of the pure type; the northern and eastern horizon is fairly well known.

Granting that the great ruins on the Chaco Canyon belong to the same people as those on Mesa Verde, the question arises, Which buildings are the most ancient, those on the Mesa Verde or those on the Chaco? A correct answer to this question should reveal the cradle of the culture indicated by the pure or prehistoric type of pueblo. The author believes that the pure pueblo culture originated in the northern part of the area and migrated southward to the Chaco Valley in prehistoric times, ultimately affecting the people of the Rio Grande, where sedentary people no doubt lived before written history of the area began. The result was a mixture; the mixed population are the modern Pueblos.

In the great cliff-houses of the Mesa Verde and the extensive pueblos of the McElmo we find towers combined with pure types of pueblos, either simple or complex. In the Chaco ruins these towers are not found in this combination. To this may be added the great house type of the McElmo, also absent in the Chaco. Here there appears to be an essential difference on which the author ventures a suggestion, but which future research must elucidate.

If this pure type originated in the southern tributaries of the San Juan as the Chaco and migrated to the northern we would expect in the latter more distinctly southern objects, as shell ornaments, turquoise mosaics, and a great variety of pottery of a southern type.

The pure or unit type is believed to be autochthonous in the San Juan Basin and characteristic of a middle phase of architectural development, the highest north of Mexico. It is self-centered and has preserved its characteristics over an extensive area, influencing regions far beyond.

The evolution of this type took place in the region mentioned before the fifteenth century of the Christian era. Traces of its influence have persisted into the country of mixed pueblos down to the present time, but the architectural skill has deteriorated and shows evidence of acculturation[58] from sources outside the San Juan area where it originated.

One word in regard to the adjectives, prehistoric and historic, applied to southwestern ruins. They are relative ones and obtained from data somewhat diverse in character. Casa Grande on the Gila was called a ruin when first seen by the European. It was inhabited in prehistoric times. From documentary evidence the historian learns that certain other buildings were not inhabited at the advent of the Spaniards, and if their statements are trustworthy these also are prehistoric. Legends of modern Pueblos claim that certain other ruins were inhabited houses of their ancestors before the coming of the white man. The author sees no good reason to throw this evidence out of court without investigation because some of the incidents in it betray late introduction. Many other ruins are classified as prehistoric from the purely negative, but not decisive, evidence that no objects of European make have been found in them. The ruin Sun Temple, on the Mesa Verde, is considered prehistoric from the fact that a tree with over 360 annual rings of growth was found growing on top of its highest wall. We are justified in calling this a prehistoric ruin.

The evidences that villages, cliff-dwellings, castles and towers, and other types considered in this article antedate the advent of the white man are as follows: No historian has recorded an inhabited building of this form in this or other regions; no objects of European manufacture have been found in them, and the buildings and pottery which characterize them are different from those of any inhabited when the Spanish entered the Southwest.

The complex, which is thought to be the highest form of pueblo architecture, is composed of the following elements united: (1) Several "pure types"[59] representing a religio-sociological complexion of the inhabitants; (2) towers of various forms—round, **D**-shaped, and rectangular; (3) the great houses; (4) unit type in cave. In Cliff Palace these four types occur united in a pueblo built in a natural cave; in Mud Spring Ruin two and possibly three of these types are found in one open-air village, more spread out as site permits. In Aztec Spring and Mitchell Spring pueblos the arrangement is more defined. In the cluster at the head of South Fork of Square Tower Canyon we have all the elements united in Hovenweep House and Hovenweep Castle. Unit type House shows the single-unit type with tower near by; in Twin Towers we have the great house with cave pueblo and towers separated. Several other towers isolated from other types also occur.

The Holly Canyon group shows the types separated. The great house is represented by Holly Castle; the towers are situated on huge bowlders. The unit type of this group is represented by Holly House, the foundation of part of which has fallen, covering the ruins of another pueblo of the unit type formerly in the cave below.

The Hackberry group is also composed of three elemental types separated; the great house is represented by Hackberry House, the unit type by the cliff-dwelling below and by the pueblo on the opposite side of the gulch, and the towers by isolated towers.

A similar analysis may be made of other ruins. Sometimes the component types are united; often one type only occurs, the others being absent. The union of all is best marked in the northern tributaries of the San Juan, as at Aztec, and in the southern tributaries, as at Chaco Canyon and Chelly Canyon. These pueblos, whether in the open or in caves, belong to the pure or concentrated multiple unit type.

Some light may be shed on the probable process of consolidation of the individual units of a community house by a comparative study of the pueblos on the East Mesa of the Hopi. Hano, for instance, was settled by a group of Tanoan clans about 1710 A. D. The list of Hano clans that originally came to the East Mesa is known from legends and the present localization of their survivors has been indicated in the author's article on "The Sun's Influence on the Form of Hopi Pueblos."[60] In 1890 Hano was composed of four blocks of rooms, each housing one or more clans. Earlier there were six, one of which had fallen into disuse, a few less than the traditional number of clans. When the colonists arrived, they settled near Coyote Spring, the houses of which are now covered with drifted sand, but when they constructed their village on the mesa at the head of the trail each house of a cluster housed a clan. Increase in population, both internal and external, led to the union and enlargement of these houses so that they inclosed a central plaza. A similar growth has taken place in Sichomovi, the pueblo halfway between Walpi and Hano; first single houses, then rows of houses with terraces on the south and east sides. Some of the original houses have been deserted and rebuilt nearer the others. Thus at Hano the Katcina clan house was north and east of the chief kiva but is now in the east row.

In the same way we may suppose that in a consolidation of a community dwelling several units may have drawn together and united. There is evidence of a union of this kind in many ruins in the Southwest.

The data here published should not be interpreted to mean that the author regards the builders of the towers and great houses here described as evidences of a race other than the Indians. Indeed he believes that in both blood and culture they have left survivals among the modern Pueblos. He also does not hold that as a whole they necessarily belonged to a radically different phase of culture, notwithstanding the buildings they constructed show a greater variety of form and masonry superior to that of their descendants.

The evidences are cumulative that there existed and disappeared in a wide geographical area of the Southwest a people whose buildings differed so much from those of any other area in North America that the area in which they occur may be designated as a characteristic one.

The variety and type of buildings have a bearing on social organization. A large building composed of many units is probably but not necessarily later in time than a single house; an isolated single house would probably be of earlier construction than a collection of several single houses of the same character compactly arranged in a village; a complete consolidation of several houses of such a village into a community house would naturally be more modern than a group of isolated single houses.

City blocks postdate hamlets. Between a stage indicated by single houses and one characterized by consolidated building, there is a phase in which the buildings are grouped in clusters and are not united. We may theoretically suppose that the single house was inhabited by one social unit as a clan or family. As the food quest became more intensified and defense more urgent, social units, as indicated by single houses, would be brought together, and as the population increased the amalgamation would be more complete. This social organization, in the beginning loose, in the course of time would become more homogeneous, and as it did so the union of these separate social units would have been closer; and if we combine with that tendency the powerful stimulus of protection, we can readily see how a compact form of architecture characteristic of the buildings here described was brought about. The element of defense in the villages with scattered houses does not appear to have been very important, but might be adduced to explain the consolidation of these into large community houses.

If the growth of the large pueblos has followed the lines above indicated, and if each unit type indicates a social unit as well, we necessarily have in this growth of the community house the story of the social evolution of the Pueblo people. Clans or social units at first isolated later joined each other, intermarriage always tending to make the population more homogeneous. The social result of the amalgamation of clans seeking common defense would in time be marked. The inevitable outcome would be a breaking down of clan priesthoods or clan religions and the formation of fraternities of priesthoods recruited from several clans. This in turn would lead to a corresponding reduction and enlargement of ceremonial rooms remaining. Two kivas suffice for the ceremonies of the majority of the Rio Grande pueblos; but Cliff Palace with a population of the same size had 23 and Spruce-tree House, a much smaller cliff pueblo, had 8.

One can not fail to notice a similarity in sites of some of the great houses of the McElmo to neighboring cliff habitations and a like relation of Sun Temple to the cliff-dwellings in Fewkes Canyon in the Mesa Verde. Possibly the purpose of these great houses and Sun Temple was identical. Some of the great houses were probably granaries and Sun Temple may have been intended partly for a like use. No indications of remains of stored corn have been observed in any of these buildings, but Castañeda[61] speaks of a village of subterranean granaries ("silos") in the Rio Grande country, which is instructive in this connection.

INDEX

Page

- ACMEN RUIN, described, 29
- ANTIQUITIES, minor, 66
- ARCHITECTURE, culture areas determined by, 69
- ARCHITECTURE, PUEBLO—
- elements of, 73
- of local origin, 70
- AZTEC ARCHITECTURE, unlike that of Pueblos, 69
- AZTEC SPRING, ruins at, 23
- described by Holmes, 24
- described by Jackson, 24
- ground plan of, 26
- BEAMS, WOODEN, method of shaping, 67
- BLANCHARD RUIN, 23
- BONE, objects made of, 67
- BOWLDER CASTLE, description of, 57
- BOWLS, MORTUARY, 66
- BUG MESA RUIN, description of, 19
- BUG POINT RUIN, excavation of, showing unit type, 29
- BURIAL CUSTOMS, 66, 67
- BURIAL PLACES—
- mentioned by Morgan, 21
- near Holmes Tower, 59
- on Grass Mesa, 64
- on the Dolores, 11

- BURKHARDT RUIN. *See* MUD SPRING RUIN.
- BUTTE RUIN, description of, 32
- CANNONBALL RUIN—
- description of, 30
- structural features of, 42
- CASTLES, structural features of, 40
- CAVES—
- apparently used for storage, 60
- walled-up, 59
- CEMETERIES. *See* BURIAL PLACES.
- CEREMONIAL ROOMS, Hopi and Zuñi, not true kivas, 71
- CHACO CANYON RUINS, comparative age of, 72
- CIRCULAR RUINS—
- distribution of, 31
- structural features of, 31
- CLIFF-DWELLERS—
- culture of, 9
- region occupied by, 9
- CLIFF-DWELLINGS—
- architectural features of, 37
- classification of, 15
- double, 38
- in Lost Canyon, 40
- small, in the McElmo region, 37
- COMMUNAL DWELLINGS, 71
- preceded by "small house", 70
- social conditions indicated by, 69
- CONSOLIDATION OF UNITS, process of, 74

- CORN, CHARRED, found embedded in slag, 60
- DAVIS TOWER—
- ground plan, 55
- location of, 55
- DEPRESSIONS INDICATING KIVAS, 42
- DOVE CREEK RUINS, 28
- EIGHT MILE RUIN, masonry in, 41
- EMERSON, J. W., description of ruin by, 34
- EMERSON RUIN, description of, 33
- ENTRANCES—
- to kivas, 42
- to towers, 42
- walled-up, 57
- ERODED BOWLDER HOUSE, description of, 49
- ESCALANTE AND DOMINGUEZ, manuscript diary of, 36
- ESCALANTE RUIN, description of, 36
- FAR VIEW HOUSE, a pueblo of pure type, 15, 16
- GIBRALTAR HOUSE. *See* STRONGHOLD HOUSE.
- GILA VALLEY COMPOUNDS, 71
- allied to Mexican buildings, 67
- GOODMAN POINT RUIN, description of, 17
- GRASS MESA, cemetery on, 64
- GREAT HOUSES—
- date of construction undetermined, 43
- possible use of, 42, 76
- structural features of, 40
- HACKBERRY CANYON CLIFF-HOUSE, a "unit type", 40
- HACKBERRY CASTLE, description of, 52

- HACKBERRY GROUP, elements composing, 74
- HILL CANYON RUINS, 42
- masonry of, 42
- HOLLY CANYON—
- ground plan, 52
- ruins of, 52
- HOLLY CANYON GROUP, elements composing, 74
- HOLLY HOUSE RUINS, description of, 53
- HOLMES, W. H.—
- on probable use of towers, 42
- on tower at Mud Spring, 20
- report of, as reference work, 11
- report on ruins by, 10, 11
- slab inclosures described by, 62
- HOLMES TOWER, description of, 58
- HOPI CEREMONIAL ROOMS, not true kivas, 71
- HORSESHOE HOUSE—
- compared with Sun Temple, 54
- description of, 53
- ground plan, 54
- structural features of, 40
- HOVENWEEP CASTLE—
- description of, 47
- ground plan of, 47
- HOVENWEEP DISTRICT—
- a proposed National Monument, 44
- canyons of, containing ruins, 44
- ruins of, 44

- Hovenweep House, description of, 46
- Implements, stone, 67
- Ingersoll, Ernest, newspaper article by, 11
- Jackson, Wm. H.—
- report of, as work of reference, 11
- report of, on ruins, 10, 11
- slab inclosures described by, 62
- Johnson Ruin, description of, 18
- Keeley Towers, location of, 45
- Kidder, A. V. *See* Morley and Kidder.
- Kiva of Unit type House, architectural features of, 51
- Kivas—
- double-walled, 39
- entrances to, 42
- indicated by depressions, 42
- indicative of social units, 70
- structural features of, 37
- Lion Tower—
- description of, 55
- ground plan of, 55
- Littrell Tower. *See* Lion Tower.
- Lost Canyon cliff-houses, 40
- "Lower House," of Aztec Spring Ruin, 25, 27
- McElmo Bluff, ruins at, 60
- McElmo district—
- distinctive feature of ruins of, 15
- investigations in, of 1917, 10
- McElmo ruins, latest work on, 14

- MCLEAN BASIN—
- ground plan of ruins of, 56
- pottery found in, 56
- ruins of, described, 55
- towers of, 56
- MANCOS REGION, towers of, 58
- MASONRY—
- of Hill Canyon Ruins, 42
- skill shown in construction, 40
- varieties of, 41
- MEGALITHIC RUINS, 60
- MEGALITHS, circular structures of, 60
- MESA VERDE—
- cliff-dwellings and villages of, 9
- culture of inhabitants of, 9
- MESA VERDE RUINS, comparative age of, 72
- METATES—
- found at Surouaro, 17
- with skeletal remains, 67
- MEXICAN TRIBES AND THE PUEBLOS, relation between, 69
- MITCHELL, H. L., notes contributed by, 11
- MITCHELL SPRING RUIN, description of, 19
- MITCHELL SPRING VILLAGE, origin of the name, 12
- MONOLITHS IN WALLS, 30
- MONTEZUMA VALLEY, distinctive feature of ruins in, 15
- MOOREHEAD, WARREN K., ruins described by, 12
- MORGAN, L. H.—
- investigation of ruins by, 10, 11

- notes of, on ruins of Mesa Verde, 11
- on Mitchell Spring Ruin, 19
- on Mud Creek village, 21
- MORLEY, S. G.—
- excavations conducted by, 30
- work of, 13
- MORLEY, S. G., and KIDDER, A. V., ruins described by, 14
- MOUNDS—
- near Mummy Lake, 15
- of Mud Spring Ruin, 21
- MUD SPRING RUIN, description of, 20
- MUMMY LAKE MOUNDS, 15
- NELSON, N. C., on Pueblo ruins, 17
- NEWBERRY, J. S., on Surouaro, 17
- NORDENSKIÖLD, BARON G., work of, 13
- OAK SPRING HOUSE, description of, 29
- OLD SPANISH TRAIL, route of, 36, 68
- OPEN-AIR RUINS OF DOVE CREEK, 28
- PARKER, GORDON, assistance of, 40
- PICTOGRAPHS—
- colored, 65
- covered with plaster, 65
- incised on stone, 65
- near Ruin 5, 49
- near slab inclosures, 63
- PIERSON LAKE RUIN. *See* SQUAW POINT RUIN.
- PILASTERS LACKING IN TOWERS, 42
- PLASTERING, interiors covered with, 41

- POTTERY—
- culture areas determined by, 69
- description of, 66
- PRUDDEN, T. MITCHELL—
- articles by, on ruins of San Juan watershed, 12
- excavations conducted by, 19
- on towers as part of composite ruins, 44
- PUEBLO ARCHITECTURE—
- elements of complex, 73
- of local origin, 70
- PUEBLO CULTURE, direction of its migration, 72
- PUEBLO TRIBES, origin of, 69
- "PURE TYPE" defined, 16
- RESERVOIR GROUP, named by J. Ward Emerson, 34
- RESERVOIRS, INDIAN—
- crossed by Old Bluff Road, 45
- natural and artificial, 64
- ROAD CANYON, formerly called the Wickyup, 57
- ROOMS, with megalithic walls, 15
- RUIN 3, description of, 48
- RUIN 4, description of, 49
- RUIN 5, description of, 49
- RUIN 6, description of, 49
- RUIN 7. *See* ERODED BOWLDER HOUSE.
- RUIN 8. *See* TWIN TOWERS.
- RUIN 9, description of, 50
- RUIN 10. *See* UNIT TYPE HOUSE.
- RUIN 11. *See* STRONGHOLD HOUSE.

- RUIN CANYON—
  - duplication of name misleading, 45
  - ruin in, 30
  - unit type houses of, 40
- RUINS—
  - classification of, 14
  - evidences of age of, 73
- SAND CANYON—
  - cliff-dwellings in, 38
  - scaffold in, 38
  - tower in, 57
- SCAFFOLD FOR LOOKOUT, 38
- SEMICIRCULAR RUINS, description of, 22
- SLAB INCLOSURES—
  - described by Jackson, 62
  - described by Holmes, 62
- SLAB STRUCTURES—
  - box-like, 60
  - circular, 60
  - pottery found near, 61
  - theories concerning, 61
- "SMALL HOUSE" TYPE OF ARCHITECTURE, 70
- SOCIAL ORGANIZATION, relation between architecture and, 75
- "SPANISH TRAIL." *See* OLD SPANISH TRAIL.
- SQUARE TOWER CANYON—
  - classification of ruins in, 46
  - directions for reaching, 45
  - map of, 45

- new name for Ruin Canyon, 45
- SQUAW POINT RUIN, described, 28
- STONE ARCH HOUSE, location of, 38
- STRONGHOLD HOUSE, description of, 52
- SUN DIAL PALACE, named by J. Ward Emerson, 34
- SUN TEMPLE—
- discovery of, 10
- evidence of age of, 73
- possible use of, 76
- unique ground plan of, 42
- SUROUARO—
- description of, 16
- named by Newberry, 12
- signification of name, 17
- TOWERS—
- **D**-shaped, 44
- date of construction undetermined, 43
- entrance to, 42
- entrance walled up, 57
- forms of, 43
- of Holly Canyon, 52
- of McLean Basin, 56
- of Mancos region, 58
- of Sand Canyon, 57
- of Wickyup Canyon, 57
- possible use of, 42
- structural features of, 40
- windows absent in, 42

- TOWERS AND GREAT HOUSES—
- form and construction of, 15
- situation of, 15
- "TRIPLE-WALLED TOWER"—
- at Mud Spring Ruin, 20
- condition of, in 1881, 21
- visited by Holmes, 11
- TWIN TOWERS—
- description of, 50
- ground plan of, 50
- UNIT TYPE—
- defined, 16, 39
- described by Prudden, 12
- origin of, 72
- unlike small house of Little Colorado, 70
- UNIT TYPE HOUSE—
- description of, 50
- ground plan of, 51
- UNIT TYPE HOUSES—
- in cave, 39
- in Hackberry Canyon, 40
- "UPPER HOUSE" of Aztec Spring Ruin, 25, 26, 27
- VILLAGES—
- defined, 16
- essential features of, 14, 16
- WEAPONS, iron, 68
- WICKYUP CANYON—
- description of, 57

- towers in, <u>57</u>
- WOLLEY RANCH RUIN, description of, <u>22</u>
- WOOD CANYON RUINS, description of, <u>32</u>
- YELLOW JACKET CANYON—
- formerly known as Hovenweep, <u>57</u>
- investigations in, <u>10</u>
- towers of, <u>54</u>
- ZUÑI CEREMONIAL ROOMS NOT TRUE KIVAS, <u>71</u>

PLATE 1

a, BUTTE RUIN

b, AZTEC SPRING RUIN

c, SUROUARO,
YELLOW JACKET SPRING RUIN

(Photographs by Jacob Wirsula)

PLATE 2

a, BLANCHARD RUIN

b, BLANCHARD RUIN,
MOUND 2

c, SUROUARO,
YELLOW JACKET SPRING RUIN

(Photographs by Jacob Wirsula)

PLATE 3

a, ACMEN RUIN

(Photograph by T. G. Lemmon)

b, MUD SPRING RUIN

(Photograph by Jacob Wirsula)

PLATE 4

a, BUILDING ON ROCK PINNACLE,
NEAR STONE ARCH,
SAND CANYON

b, STONE ARCH,
SAND CANYON

(Photographs by J. Walter Fewkes)

PLATE 5

a, TOWER IN SAND CANYON

b, UNIT TYPE HOUSE
IN SAND CANYON

(Photographs by T. G. Lemmon)

PLATE 6

a, STONE ARCH HOUSE,
SAND CANYON

b, CLIFF-HOUSE,
SHOWING BROKEN CORNER

(Photographs by Jacob Wirsula)

PLATE 7

a, SCAFFOLD IN SAND CANYON

b, STORAGE CIST
IN MANCOS VALLEY

c, PICTOGRAPHS NEAR
UNIT TYPE HOUSE IN CAVE

(Photographs by T. G. Lemmon)

PLATE 8

DOUBLE CLIFF-DWELLING,
SAND CANYON

(Photograph by T. G. Lemmon)

PLATE 9

a, CLIFF-DWELLING
UNDER HORSESHOE RUIN

b, CLIFF-DWELLING,
RUIN CANYON

(Photographs by Jacob Wirsula)

PLATE 10

a, KIVA OF CLIFF RUIN, LOST CANYON

b, CLIFF RUIN,
LOST CANYON

(Photographs by Gordon Parker)

PLATE 11

a, SQUARE TOWER IN
SQUARE TOWER CANYON

b, TOWER IN McLEAN BASIN

c, RUIN IN HILL CANYON,
UTAH

(Photographs by T. G. Lemmon)

PLATE 12

HEAD OF SOUTH FORK,
SQUARE TOWER CANYON

(Photograph by Geo. L. Beam. Courtesy of the Denver & Rio Grande
Railroad)

PLATE 13

NORTH FORK OF SQUARE TOWER CANYON, LOOKING WEST

b, Hovenweep House.   a, Hovenweep Castle.
d, Tower on point at junction   c, Tower No. 9.
of North and South Forks.
f, Unit type House   e, Twin Towers.

(Photograph by Geo. L. Beam. Courtesy of the Denver & Rio Grande Railroad)

PLATE 14

a, HOVENWEEP HOUSE AND HOVENWEEP CASTLE, FROM THE SOUTH

b, HOVENWEEP CASTLE,
FROM THE WEST

c, HOVENWEEP CASTLE,
FROM THE SOUTH

(Photographs by Jacob Wirsula)

PLATE 15

a, WEST END OF TWIN TOWER,
SHOWING SMALL CLIFF-HOUSE

(Photograph by J. Walter Fewkes)

b, TWIN TOWERS,
SQUARE TOWER CANYON,
FROM THE SOUTH

(Photograph by Jacob Wirsula)

c, TOWER 4,
JUNCTION OF NORTH AND SOUTH FORKS,
SQUARE TOWER CANYON

(Photograph by Jacob Wirsula)

PLATE 16

a, HOVENWEEP CASTLE, WITH SLEEPING UTE MOUNTAIN,
SOUTH FORK, SQUARE TOWER CANYON

b, ENTRANCE TO SOUTH FORK,
SQUARE TOWER CANYON

(Photographs by Geo. L. Beam. Courtesy of the Denver & Rio Grande Railroad)

PLATE 17

STRONGHOLD HOUSE,
SQUARE TOWER CANYON

(Photograph by Geo. L. Beam. Courtesy of the Denver & Rio Grande Railroad)

PLATE 18

a, HEAD OF HOLLY CANYON

b, SOUTH SIDE OF HOVENWEEP CASTLE,
SQUARE TOWER CANYON

(Photographs by Geo. L. Beam. Courtesy of the Denver & Rio Grande Railroad)

PLATE 19

a, HOLLY CANYON GROUP,
FROM THE EAST

(Photograph by Jacob Wirsula)

b, GREAT HOUSE AT HEAD OF HOLLY CANYON,
FROM THE NORTH

(Photograph by T. G. Lemmon)

c, UNIT TYPE RUIN,
FROM THE EAST

(Photograph by T. G. Lemmon)

PLATE 20

a, GREAT HOUSE AT HEAD OF HOLLY CANYON,
FROM THE SOUTH

b, RUIN B AT HEAD OF HOLLY CANYON,
FROM THE WEST

c, GREAT HOUSE
AT HEAD OF HOLLY CANYON

(Photographs by Jacob Wirsula)

PLATE 21

a, GREAT HOUSE,
HOLLY CANYON

b, STRONGHOLD HOUSE AND TWIN TOWERS,
SQUARE TOWER CANYON

(Photographs by Geo. L. Beam. Courtesy of the Denver & Rio Grande Railroad)

PLATE 22

a, HOVENWEEP CASTLE

b, SOUTHERN PART OF CANNONBALL RUIN, McELMO CANYON

(Photographs by T. G. Lemmon)

PLATE 23

a, SQUARE TOWER WITH ROUNDED CORNERS,
HOLLY CANYON

(Photograph by Jacob Wirsula)

b, HOLLY TOWER
IN HOLLY CANYON

(Photograph by Jacob Wirsula)

c, HORSESHOE HOUSE

(Photograph by T. G. Lemmon)

PLATE 24

a, HORSESHOE RUIN

(Photograph by Jacob Wirsula)

b, BOWLDER CASTLE,
ROAD (WICKYUP) CANYON

(Photograph by T. G. Lemmon)

PLATE 25

a, CLOSED DOORWAY
IN BOWLDER CASTLE,
ROAD (WICKYUP) CANYON

(Photograph by J. Walter Fewkes)

b, BROKEN-DOWN ROUND TOWER,
SQUARE TOWER CANYON

(Photograph by Jacob Wirsula)

PLATE 26

a, NORTH SIDE OF TOWER,
SQUARE TOWER CANYON

(Photograph by Jacob Wirsula)

b, **D**-SHAPED TOWER NEAR DAVIS RANCH, YELLOW JACKET CANYON

(Photograph by Jacob Wirsula)

c, MODEL OF TOWERS IN McLEAN BASIN

(Photograph by De Lancey Gill)

PLATE 27

ROUND TOWER AND **D**-SHAPED TOWER
IN McLEAN BASIN

(Photograph by J. Walter Fewkes)

PLATE 28

a, **D**-SHAPED TOWER
IN McLEAN BASIN,
SHOWING CROSS SECTION OF WALL

b, ROUND TOWER
IN McLEAN BASIN,
SHOWING STANDING STONE SLAB

(Photographs by J. Walter Fewkes)

PLATE 29

a, HOLMES TOWER, MANCOS CANYON

b, LION TOWER,
YELLOW JACKET CANYON

(Photographs by T. G. Lemmon)

PLATE 30

a, TOWER ABOVE CAVATE STOREHOUSES,
MANCOS CANYON BELOW BRIDGE

b, TOWER ON MESA BETWEEN ERODED CLIFFS
AND BRIDGE OVER MANCOS CANYON
ON CORTEZ SHIP-ROCK ROAD

(Photographs by T. G. Lemmon)

PLATE 31

a, TOWER ABOVE CAVATE STOREHOUSES,
MANCOS CANYON BELOW BRIDGE

b, ERODED SHALE FORMATION
IN WHICH ARE SMALL WALLED
CAVATE STOREHOUSES

(Photographs by T. G. Lemmon)

PLATE 32

a, RESERVOIR NEAR PICKET CORRAL, SHOWING RETAINING WALL

b, KIVA, UNIT TYPE HOUSE, SQUARE TOWER CANYON

(Photographs by T. G. Lemmon)

PLATE 33

PICTOGRAPHS,
YELLOW JACKET CANYON

Footnotes:

[1] Ancient Ruins in Southwestern Colorado. Rept. U.S. Geol. Surv. Terr. (Hayden Survey) for 1874, Washington, 1876.

[2] The situation of a spring near Hovenweep Castle indicates that the Great House may be the Hovenweep Castle of early writers.

[3] Report on the ancient ruins of Southwestern Colorado. Tenth Ann. Rept. U. S. Geol. Surv. Terr. (Hayden Survey) for 1876, Washington, 1879.

[4] The Prehistoric Ruins of the San Juan Watershed in Utah, Arizona, Colorado, and New Mexico., Amer. Anthrop., n. s. vol. v, no. 2, 1903.

[5] The Circular Kivas of Small Ruins in the San Juan Watershed. Amer. Anthrop., n. s. vol. xvi, no. 1, 1914.

[6] Memoirs Amer. Anthrop. Asso., vol. v, no. 1, 1918.

[7] Amer. Anthrop., n. s. vol. v, no. 2, 1903.

[8] The Excavation of the Cannonball Ruins in Southwestern Colorado. Amer. Anthrop., n. s. vol. x, no. 4, 1908.

[9] The Archaeology of McElmo Canyon, Colorado. El Palacio, vol. iv, no. 4, Santa Fe, 1917.

[10] The dimensions of buildings and towers given in this article are welcome additions to our knowledge, but from lack of ground plans one can not fully determine the arrangement of rooms designated in individual ruins.

[11] A Prehistoric Mesa Verde Pueblo and its People. Smithson. Rept. for 1916, pp. 461-488, 1917. Far View House—a Pure Type of Pueblo Ruin. Art and Archaeology, vol. vi, no. 3, 1917.

[12] The situation of the cemetery, one of the characters of Prudden's "unit type," appears constant in one kiva buildings, but is variable in the pure type, and, as shown in the author's application of the unit type to the crowded condition in Spruce-tree House and other cliff-houses, does not occur in the same position as in pueblos of the pure type open to the sky.

[13] In his valuable study, Pueblo Ruins of the Galisteo Basin, New Mexico (Anthrop. Papers of the Amer. Mus. Nat. Hist., vol. XV, pt. 1, 1914), Mr. Nelson figures (Plan I, B) an embedded circular kiva in what he calls the "historic part" of the Galisteo Ruin, but does not state how he distinguishes the historic from the prehistoric part of this building. The other kivas at Galisteo are few in number and not embedded, but situated outside the house masses as in historic pueblos.

[14] Report of the exploring expedition from Santa Fe, New Mexico, to the Junction of the Grand and Green Rivers of the Great Colorado of the West in 1859, under the command of Capt. J. N. Macomb, p. 88, Washington, 1876.

[15] Memoirs Amer. Anthrop. Asso., vol. V, no. 1, 1918.

[16] Houses and House-life of the American Aborigines. Cont. N. Amer. Ethn., vol. IV, pp. 189-190, 1831.

[17] Prudden excavated a unit type ruin from one of the Mitchell Spring mounds. (Amer. Anthrop., vol. XVI, no. 1, 1914.)

[18] Op. cit., pp. 398-399.

[19] Op. cit., p. 190.

[20] Although the kivas of Mud Spring Ruin have not been excavated there is little doubt from surface indications that they belong to the unit type.

[21] Tenth Ann. Rept. U. S. Geol. Surv. Terr. (Hayden Survey) for 1876, pl. xlviii, fig. 2, 1879.

[22] Rept. U. S. Geol. Survey Terr. (Hayden Survey) for 1874, Washington, 1876.

[23] Op. cit.

[24] Op. cit., pp. 377-378.

[25] Op. cit., p. 400.

[26] Op. cit., pl. xl.

[27] Mr. Van Kleeck, of Denver, has offered this ruin to the Public Parks Service for permanent preservation. It is proposed to rename it the Yucca House National Monument.

[28] Amer. Anthrop., n. s. vol. x, no. 4, pp. 596-610, 1908.

[29] Op. cit., pp. 428-429.

[30] It is premature to declare that the kivas in circular ruins do not belong to the vaulted-roofed type simply from want of observation to that effect. In Penasco Blanco and other ruins of the Chaco Canyon group, as shown in ground plans, they appear to be embedded in secular rooms. Additional studies of the architectural features of circular pueblos are desirable.

[31] The letter referring to the circular ruin near Dolores was prepared by Mr. Emerson, the discoverer of this ruin, and was transmitted to the Smithsonian Institution as part of a phase of cooperative work with the Forest Service, by Mr. Gordon Parker, superintendent of the Montezuma Forest Reserve.

[32] Also see detailed map of construction of Sun Dial Palace (fig. 4).

[33] Fewkes, J. W., The First Pueblo Ruin in Colorado Mentioned in Spanish Documents. Science, vol. xlvi, Sept. 14, 1917.

[34] Diario y Dereotero de las nuevas descubrimientos de tierras a los r'bos N. N. OE. OE. del Nuevo Mexico por los R. R. P. P. Fr. Silvester Velez Escalante, Fr. Francisco Atanacio Dominguez, 1776. (Vide Sen. Ex. Doc. 33d Congress, No. 78, pt. 3, pp. 119-127.)

[35] Attention may be called to the fact that often we find very commodious caves without correspondingly large cliff-houses, even in the Mesa Verde.

[36] Sun Temple, however, is a seeming exception and follows the McElmo rule of proximity; several large cliff-dwellings occur under the cliff on which this mysterious building stands.

[37] Taken from a point across the canyon, the only one from which both houses can be included in the same photograph.

[38] For a good example of cliff-houses at different levels, see Cliff-Dwellings in Fewkes Canyon, Mesa Verde National Park, Holmes Anniversary Volume.

[39] Antiquities of the Mesa Verde National Park: Spruce-tree House. Bull. 41, Bur. Amer. Ethn., 1909.

[40] The name Ruin Canyon, often applied also to Square Tower Canyon, is retained for this canyon.

[41] Smithson. Misc. Colls., vol. 68, no. 1, 1917.

[42] Our knowledge of the entrances into kivas of the vaulted-roofed type is not all that could be desired. Kiva D of Spruce-tree House has a passageway opening through the floor of an adjacent room, and Kiva A of Cliff Palace has the same feature. Doctor Prudden has found lateral entrances from kivas into adjoining rooms in his unit type pueblo. The majority of cliff-dwellers' kivas show no evidence of lateral entrances.

[43] Mr. Jackson, op. cit., p. 415, regarded it likely that the towers were "lookouts or places of refuge for the sheep herders who brought their sheep or goats up here to graze, just as the Navajos used to and as the Utes do at the present time." This explanation is impossible, for there is no evidence that the builders of the towers had either sheep or goats, the Navajos and the Utes obtaining both from the Spaniards.

[44] The tower figured by Prudden (Amer. Anthrop., n. s. vol. v, no. 2, pl. xviii, fig. 2) as a "round tower" is really semicircular, as shown in the ground plan (fig. 14) here published.

[45] Ibid., pp. 241, 263, 273.

[46] Among the older photographs seen by the author are those of W. H. Jackson, prints of which are on exhibition in the State Historical Museum at Denver, Colo.

[47] The "unit type" was first recognized by Doctor Prudden in his illuminating studies of the pueblos of the San Juan Basin. The author was the first to point out its existence in cliff-houses of the same area.

[48] Circular Kivas in San Juan Watershed. Amer. Anthrop., n. s. vol. 16, no. 1, 1914.

[49] Excavation of the Cannonball Ruins in southwestern Colorado. Amer. Anthrop., n. s. vol. x, no. 4, 1908.

[50] Explorations in southeastern Utah. Amer. Journ. Archæol., 2d ser., vol. xiv, no. 3, 1910.

[51] This tower is reputed to be the home of a mountain lion, hence the name Lion House.

[52] A good figure of these cavate rooms is given by Holmes, op. cit. Comparing the photograph with his figure it appears that their surrounding shale has worn away somewhat in the last four decades.

[53] Tenth Ann. Rept. U. S. Geol. Surv. (Hayden Survey) for 1876, p. 414, 1879.

[54] The use of these objects as heirlooms in the Antelope altar of the Hopi supports the tradition of the Snake people that their ancestors brought them from the San Juan.

[55] Temples of Quetzalcoatl, the Plumed Serpent Sun God, are circular buildings like towers.

[56] The likeness of the Mesa Verde cliff-houses to the pueblos of Chaco Canyon was long ago suggested by Nordenskiöld. The excavation of Far View House proved that suggestion to be true.

[57] This subject is treated at length in my report on Casa Grande in the Twenty-eighth Annual Report of the Bureau of American Ethnology.

[58] These acculturation modifications due to Hispanic influences in modern pueblos are too well marked to need more than a mention.

[59] The author uses the words "pure type" instead of "unit type" as a general term to denote "one-unit types," "two-unit types," "three-unit types," etc.

[60] Amer. Anthrop., n. s. vol. viii, no. 1, 1906.

[61] Fourteenth Ann. Rept. Bur. Amer. Ethn., pt. 1, p. 523. This village is spoken of as "lately destroyed;" in other words it was a ruin in 1540.

Milton Keynes UK
Ingram Content Group UK Ltd.
UKHW050238220624
444555UK00005BA/450